Hindu Astrology

A Guide to Vedic Astrology, the 12 Zodiac Signs and Nakshatras

Your Free Gift (only available for a limited time)

Thanks for getting this book! If you want to learn more about various spirituality topics, then join Mari Silva's community and get a free guided meditation MP3 for awakening your third eye. This guided meditation mp3 is designed to open and strengthen ones third eye so you can experience a higher state of consciousness. Simply visit the link below the image to get started.

https://spiritualityspot.com/meditation

Contents

Part 1: Vedic Astrology

The Ultimate Guide to Hindu Astrology and the 12 Zodiac Signs

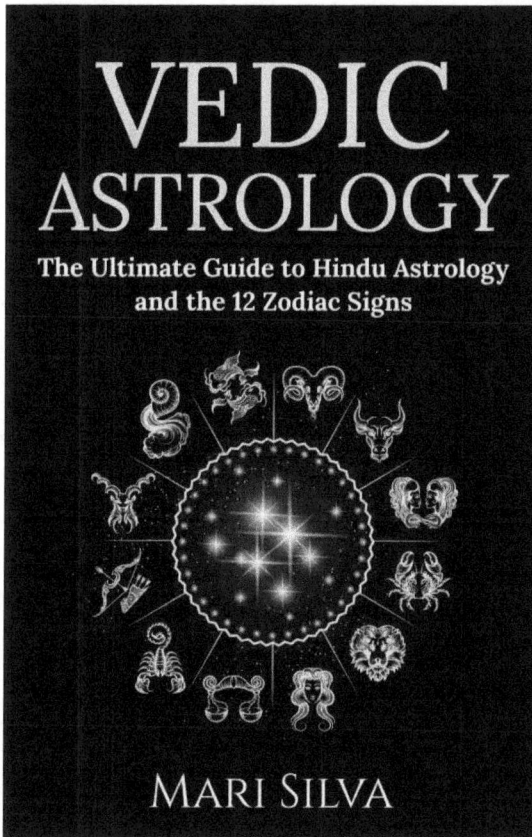

Introduction

Vedic Astrology or Jyotishya is a gift to the world from ancient India, predating the Christian era. This science is not experimentally contrived but perceived through the power of enlightened vision by ancient sages and seers, notably among them, Sage Parashara, believed to be the original author of the Vedic texts.

Vedic Astrology is the need of the hour considering the confusing milieu that boggles the modern world. Despite the apparent achievement of high levels of modern materialistic comfort, we are still doggedly pursuing sustainable happiness. The primary reason for this dichotomy is that we don't seem to know or accept that each of us is unique and has different needs and life purposes.

Vedic Astrology is a tool of wisdom gifted to us by the ancient seers of India to help us understand this uniqueness of our individuality so we can follow the path of our personal life purpose.

This book is written with the view of teaching the basics of Vedic Astrology to the beginner. And yet, people who already have a reasonably sound knowledge of this fascinating and vast subject will benefit from it. The book contains numerous aspects of Vedic Astrology within its covers. Knowing you can access a wide variety of topics without having to shift from one book to another is a great advantage for both new and experienced learners.

Starting from the most basic part, namely a simple yet powerful introduction to this ancient but timeless subject - right up to the complex and layered topic of Ashtakavarga tables, this book is great for all those interested in Vedic Astrology. Furthermore, this book is up-to-date and comprehensive, giving both beginners and experts the perfect combination to learn and refresh their knowledge on the various subtopics of Jyotishya.

A beginner can start from Chapter 1 and learn step-by-step as the complexity increases. An expert could just flip through the table of contents and choose a topic he or she needs to access immediately and clear any doubt arising at the moment. Therefore, although it is a beginner book, it can be a valuable addition for an expert too.

Chapter 1: Introduction to Ancient Vedic Astrological Texts

Centuries ago, India's ancient sages and rishis had spoken about the now-popular concept of self-awareness, which is proven to be highly beneficial for the growth and development of an individual. The ancient seers said, "Self-knowledge is the basis of all knowledge." The more you know about yourself, the better your ability to assimilate external knowledge learned from books, teachers, guides, and mentors.

Learning about yourself includes knowing the effects of the planetary system on your life, which is what Vedic Astrology or Jyotishya is about. Jyotish, in Sanskrit, translates as "the science of light." It is an important limb of the Vedas, the ancient sacred texts of India, and the Sanatana Dharma, which the western world knows as Hinduism. Jyotish is referred to with other names and different spellings, including:

- Jyotisha
- Jyotishya

- Hindu Astrology

- Vedic Astrology

- Indian Astrology

The term *Hindu Astrology* has been in use since the beginning of the 19th century. Vedic Astrology gained prominence, especially in the western world, around the 1970s, thanks to Yoga and Ayurveda's spread. Vedanga Jyotishya is one of the earliest astronomical texts found within the Vedas, dated many centuries before Christ's birth.

Vedic Astrology is based on two primary concepts in Hinduism, namely karma and rebirth. Simplistically put, in Hinduism, the law of Karma states we live and work within certain parameters and limitations created by actions or karma performed in our previous lifetimes. Therefore, it is possible to predict our future through Vedic Astrology, which has the power to demonstrate which of the previous karma will come to fruition in the present lifetime.

And it paves the path to spiritual development by showing how individuals can improve their quality of life through the practice of higher thoughts and better living.

History of Vedic Astrology

There are six Vedangas, the auxiliary disciplines of the Indian Vedic System of learning. These six Vedangas or branches of studies are essential for the support of Vedic rituals and education. They are:

- Shiksha (Phonetics)

- Kalpa (Ritual Canon)

- Vyakaran (Grammar)

- Nirukta (Explanation)

- Chhanda (Vedic Meter)

- Jyotishya (Astrology)

Vedanga Jyotishya is one of the earliest known texts on Vedic Astrology. The extant work is dated to the last few centuries B.C. But it is strongly believed that the Vedanga Jyotishya describes a tradition that goes back at least to 600-700 B.C.

The Vedanga Jyotishya is highly relevant to the dating of the Vedas because it depicts the winter solstice for the period around 1400 B.C. This story of the winter solstice is used to discover the antiquity of the Vedas. There are two versions of the Vedanga Jyotishya, one for the Rig Veda and a second one for the Yajur Veda. Both these recensions have the same verses except for eight extra verses in the Yajur Veda recension.

Experts believe that the description of the winter solstice around 1400 B.C. means the text was written around the same time. Other experts felt this period's narrative does not mean it was written then because it could have been recorded later. Regardless of its antiquity, Vedanga Jyotishya being a significant auxiliary discipline to the study of the Vedas, reflect the criticality of Vedic Astrology in Sanatana Dharma.

The ancient practice of Jyotishya was an important aspect of Vedic rituals, especially to determine the auspicious time and date of yogic events for optimal benefits for all concerned. In multiple Hindu scriptures like the Chandogya Upanishad and the Atharva Veda, there are warnings of demonic eclipses we should be cautious of and do the preparation needed for protection against their negative influence. Chandogya Upanishad talks of Rahu being a "shadowy" figure responsible for eclipse occurrences, an accurate analogical explanation of eclipses, according to modern science.

Today, the Sanskrit word, "*Graha*" means "planet." But "Graha" actually translates to "demon." The foundation of Vedic Astrology lies in the core principle of Sanatana Dharma, which believes there is an infallible connection between the macrocosm and the microcosm. Jyotish is like a lens through which we can gain insight about our lives and understand our extended life, which includes the bigger picture, both in the materialistic and the metaphysical world. What happens to an individual is affected by what happens in the outside world, including the vast astronomical spaces beyond the realm of humans.

Ancient Classical Texts of Vedic Astrology

Many classical texts of Vedic Astrology have been in use from ancient times to the present day. Important names that come to mind when discussing ancient texts are Parashar, Varahamihir, and Jaimini. Let us look at the most important works written by these famous authors and others.

Brihat Parashara Hora Shastra

Believed to have been created by Sage Parashara, a highly learned rishi of the ancient Vedic period, the original version of this large, extant text is supposed to have had 100 chapters. However, no one has the text in its full form. The current form has 13 chapters.

Nearly all scholars agree that the Brihat Parashara Hora Shastra is the most comprehensive and exhaustive compendium on Vedic Astrology. Without studying this, no student can hope to become an effective scholar on the subject. Without it, the student's knowledge will be half-baked, to say the least.

This book contains many important features of Vedic Astrology, including but not limited to:

- Description of planets
- Zodiac signs
- Houses
- Divisional charts

All kinds of mathematical calculations needed for Vedic Astrology students are described in meticulous detail throughout. Another noteworthy feature of this work is the availability of remedial measures for inauspicious births.

Brihat Jatak

This ancient text on Vedic Astrology is believed to have been composed and written by Varahamihira, a famous poet and scholar who was part of the legendary King Vikramaditya, who ruled around 57 B.C. Varahamihira was also a great astronomer.

He was the first one to mention ayanamsa or the shifting of the vernal equinox by exactly 50.32 seconds (which is approximated to 1-degree) every 72 years. This finds mention in Varahamihira's book Pancha Siddhantika based on India's ancient Siddhanta (the Mathematical and Astronomical Branch).

The inclusion of the ayanamsa to arrive at the 12 Zodiac signs of Vedic Astrology is one of the primary differences between Sidereal Astrology (or Vedic Astrology) and Western (or Tropical Astrology) in which this small but impactful shift is not included.

One of the biggest attractions of Brihat Jatak for scholars of Vedic Astrology is the contents of Chapter 10, "Karmajeeva," which deals with the livelihoods of individuals. This important chapter deals with the various earnings that people can have in just four shlokas (or verses). Novices get the feeling that four shlokas are insufficient for an exhaustive repertoire of livelihoods. And yet, the brevity of the chapter speaks volumes on the brilliance of Varahamihira, his immense control over the language, and the subject of Vedic Astrology.

Brihat Samhita

Considered one of the greatest classics of Vedic Astrology, Brihat Samhita was authored by Varahamihira, the same scholar who wrote Brihat Jatak. This text is used to make predictions of nations and kingdoms. It is written in two parts, namely "Pratham

Kanda" containing 57 chapters and "Dwitiya Kanda," containing 50 chapters. Varahamihira believed in the importance of having a genuine astrologer for daily life. He also explains how to identify a genuine astrologer from a fake one.

In the Brihat Samhita, there is an entire chapter titled "Vastu Vidya" dedicated to Vastu Shastra (dealing with buildings and architecture), an integral aspect of Vedic Astrology. Many modern astrologers erroneously take Vastu Shastra as being separate from Vedic Astrology. Also, the Brihat Samhita describes in detail how to predict any place's weather and climate.

Ashtakavarga Nibandh

Ashta means "eight" in Sanskrit. Therefore, Ashtakavarga Nibandh means "Eight Vargas." In this book, the ancient rishis of India explain and assess the strength of planets in transit. The ancient Indian seers discovered a unique system through the Ashtakavarga Nibandh, which helps scholars and practitioners of Astrology understand the malignant and beneficial effects of planets on humankind. Based on pure mathematical formulas, the calculation technique used here is unique and not found in any other writing.

Prithyusha, the son of Varahamihira, has said of this book, "The general aspects of planets in transit can be seen or understood elsewhere. However, the finer details can be observed only by using Ashtakavarga." In fact, the Ashtakavarga Nibandh has a mathematical formula that helps to arrive at the longevity of the native (or the individual whose horoscope is being analyzed).

It teaches the astrological practitioner to use the Ashtakavarga in different situations and in different charts, including the birth chart, Horary chart, Divisional chart, Varsha Kundali (or the annual life pattern), and more. Scholars believe there is no content other than Ashtakavarga Nibandh to arrive at an accurate prediction scientifically and mathematically.

Phaladeepika

Phaladeepika is another important passage written by Mantreswara, a prolific author who is believed to have been born in a family of Namboodari Brahmins (a prominent Hindu sect in the southern parts of India) around the 13th century, though some historians believe lived in the 16th century.

The exact dates of his birth and death are not known. At the end of this work, Mantreswara writes that he resided in Shalivati, the present-day district of Tirunelveli of Tamil Nadu, a Southern India state, which is a primary reason for the high popularity of the text in the southern parts of India.

This book deserves to be treated alongside other great ancient works like Brihat Parashara Hora Shastra, Jatak Parijata, Brihat Jataka, etc. This comprehensive work covers nearly all aspects of human life, and its information ranges from the very basic to very advanced.

Saravali

Written by Kalyan Varma, a prolific Sanskrit author of the 10th century, Saravali is treated on par with Brihat Parashar Hora Shastra, Brihat Jataka, and Sarvarth Chintamani. Kalyan Varma was a well-known astrologer and the king of Vyaghrapada believed to be in present-day Madhya Pradesh, a state in Central India. Saravali is an elaborate commentary on all the Vedic Astrology books studied and mastered by Kalyan Varma.

Sarvartha Chintamani

Believed to have been written in the 13th century by Venkatesha Sharma, Sarvartha Chintamani, in Sanskrit, translates to "Gem of Superior Desires and Thoughts." Containing just 17 chapters, it is one of the most popular and most-often cited books on Vedic Astrology. The most important chapters followed closely in this book deal with the yoga-formation of planets and these yogas' outcomes. It also describes the effects of each house in the natal chart, including these elements:

- Description of the planets
- Their effects
- The lifespan of the individual
- Prosperity

This text gives practical and valuable comments relating to placing the 12 houses on an individual's birth chart. It then moves on to describe the astrological explanations on the position of each house and its impacts on the individual. Sarvartha Chintamani also expands Varahamihira's thoughts on the profession of Vedic Astrology.

Jatak Parijaat

This fairly exhaustive work on Vedic Astrology is authored by Sri Vaidyanatha Dikshita, the son of another great scholar, Venkatadri. This work finds a place of honor along with the above three ancient texts and is also prescribed as a textbook for all examinations conducted on Jyotishya. It contains detailed instructions and sections on various essential aspects, including Yogas, Ayurdaya, Ashtakavarga, Vimshottari, Kalachakra Dasha, Stri Jataka, and more. Translated into multiple Indian languages, this monumental book is originally in Sanskrit and is held in high esteem by Indian astrologers all over the country.

Sri Vaidyanatha Dikshita lived in the 15th century and based highly respected work on various ancient texts, including Brihat Parashara Hora Shastra, Brihat Jataka, Saravali, Sarvatha Chintamani, and more. There are 18 chapters in this book covering the entire range of Vedic Astrology, according to the principles of Sage Parashara.

Branches of Vedic Astrology

Three broad categories include:

1. **Siddhanta** - The Siddhanta branch which deals with astronomy and its astrological applications

2. **Samhita** - The branch that handles Mundane Astrology dealing with the prediction of events related to countries. The Samhita branch deals with predicting events like earthquakes, wars, political matters, finances and economics of the country, etc.

3. **Hora** - The Hora (or Predictive) branch is further divided into more branches

The Hora branch is divided into:

- **Jatak Shastra** - Also called Hora Shastra, which deals with predictions based on individual horoscopes or Kundali, the Sanskrit term for horoscope.

- **Muhurat or Muhurtha** - Referred to as Electional Astrology, this branch of Hora Shastra deals with the selection of auspicious and beneficial times for important events for optimal fruition from life activities.

- **Swar Shastra** - Called Phonetical Astrology, this sub-branch deals with predictions based on names and sounds.

- **Prashna Shastra** - Also called Horary Astrology, this sub-branch of Hora Shastra deals with predictions based on the time when the person asks the queries or questions.

- **Ankajyotishya or Kabala** - Called Numerology, this branch deals with predictions based on numbers

- **Nadi Astrology** - This branch works with ancient treatises and texts that have detailed predictions for individuals.

• **Tajik Shastra** - Also called Varsha Phala, this sub-branch of Hora Shastra deals with astrology based on annual solar returns.

• **Jaimini Sutras** - This is a non-conventional branch of Hora Shastra that uses texts written by an ancient Indian astrologer, Acharya Jaimini. He used different but equally accurate astrological methods based on mathematics and astronomy. His works are categorized under a separate branch.

• **Nast jatak** - This branch deals with recovering and/or reconstructing lost horoscopes.

• **Streejatak** - This branch deals exclusively with astrology for female natives.

Now that you have a basic idea of the history and the historical contents of Vedic Astrology, you can learn what has been said about the nine planets and their effects on human life, both collectively and individually.

Chapter 2: The Stellar Kingdom: The Story of the Nine Planets

In Vedic Astrology, the nine heavenly bodies who are worshipped as deities and rule over the 12 zodiac signs are called Navagraha, which translates to "nine planets." The Navagraha or the nine planets include:

- Surya, the Sun
- Chandra, the Moon
- Mangala or Guja, Mars
- Buddha, Mercury
- Brihaspati or Guru, Jupiter
- Shukra, Venus
- Shani, Saturn
- Rahu, the shadow heavenly body (also known as a planet or Graha in Vedic Astrology) associated with the north lunar mode

• Ketu, the shadow planet associated with the south lunar mode

Let us look at each of these nine planets in detail, which is an essential lesson to understand Vedic Astrology.

Surya, the Sun

The Sun or Surya in Sanskrit is the star at the center of our solar system and the largest heavenly body in it. With a diameter of around 1.4 million kilometers, it is primarily made up of hydrogen and helium. Over 99% of the total mass of our solar structure is held by the Sun. The mean distance between the Sun and our planet is about 140 million kilometers. As it is stationary and at the center of our solar system, it never seems retrograde.

The Sun is the king in Vedic Astrology and is considered a royal planet. Surya represents many things, including:

• Our soul

• Willpower

• Paternal relations, especially father, called Pitrukaraka (planet connected with a father)

• The king and other high officials

Surya's color is red, which reflects his hot and angry nature. The metal is gold (like his golden rays), and his gem is ruby. He represents the eastern direction. The Sun stays in each Zodiac sign or Rashi for one month and takes 12 months or one year to complete the full circle of the Zodiac.

The Sun's movement is more or less fixed. Multiple Hindu festivals are celebrated according to the entry of the Sun into the various Rashis. For example, it enters Capricorn or Makar Rashi on January 14th, and this day is celebrated every year as Makar Sankranti. Similarly, on April 13th or 14th, the Sun enters Mesha Rashi or the Aries, and that day is celebrated as Baishakhi or New Year's Day.

Surya in Hindu Mythologyin Hindu Tradition - Surya's story, according to Hindu mythology, is very interesting. His world is known as Suryaloka and is next to the earth or bhumandala. Surya was married to Sanjana, the daughter of the celestial architect, Vishvakarma. Surya and Sanjana had three children: Vaivasvata, Yama, and Yami. Yama is the god of death. There was marital discord between the couple because Sanjana couldn't face her husband's intense heat.

One day, Sanjana left for her father's abode, leaving behind Chaaya (shadow), her body double. After spending time in her father's place, Sanjana left there too. She took on the shape of a mare and went into the mountains to meditate and pray. Surya was unaware of these arrangements made by his wife. He continued to live with Chaaya, and she gave birth to three more children: Savarni, Shani, and Taapti.

One day, Surya came to know of everything. He went in search of Sanjana and found her deep in prayer in the form of a mare. Surya took on the shape of a horse and wooed his wife, which resulted in the birth of the horse-headed twin called Ashwini Kumaras, who became the celestial physicians.

When Sanjana told her husband she couldn't handle the intensity of his heat, he divided his entire power into sixteen parts, which all became heavenly bodies, including the earth. The sun was left with one-sixteenth part of the intensity he originally had, after which Sanjana went back to live with him.

Surya's charioteer's name is Arun, and it was pulled by seven horses whose colors were the same as those in a rainbow. A highly powerful Hindu dynasty known as Suryavanshi is believed to be descendants of the Sun God. The first king of the Suryavanshi Dynasty was Ikshavku. Lord Rama, believed to be an avatar of Lord Vishnu, was born in this divine lineage. Surya, the Sun God, is known by multiple other names, including:

- Ravi, which translates to "praised and worshipped by all".
- Aditya, son of Aditi
- Surya, the supreme light or guide
- Bhanu, a ray of light or the shining one
- Arka, the radiant one
- Bhaskar, the illuminator
- Mitra, everyone's friend
- Marichi, starlight or rays of light
- Sahasranshu, one with thousand rays
- Savita, the one who purifies
- Pushan, the one who nourishes
- Khag, the one who stimulates the senses
- Prabhakar, the crater of shining light
- Martanda, the one who sprung from a lifeless egg
- Chitrabhanu, the lord of flames
- Divakar, the creator of Day
- Hiranyagarbhaya, the one with the golden womb

Important astrological facts about the sun - The temperament of Surya is steady and fixed. His primary quality is Sattva Guna. He belongs to the Kshatriya or Warrior Caste. Surya's nature is malefic and cruel. His strength is displayed when he is in the tenth house of a native's birth chart, and his weak position is when he is in the fourth house.

His natural astrological house is the fifth house. He rules Leo. His exaltation sign is Aries (or Mesha Rashi), and the sign of debilitation is Libra (or Tula Rashi). Surya's friends are Chandra, Guru, and Mangala. His enemies are Shukra and Shani. Sun is neutral with Buddha. The Nakshatras he governs are Krittika, Uttara Phalguni, and Uttarashada.

Positive keywords for Surya are vitality, creativity, confidence, leadership, and generosity. Negative keywords for the Sun are cruelty, arrogance, pomposity, conceit, and aggression. Surya is the controller of the prana or life force and imparts life-giving properties to all our organs. The planet's position in the birth chart plays an important part in the health of the native. Heart problems are primarily due to the affliction of Surya or Leo, the Zodiac sign he rules.

Chandra, the Moon

The Moon is the only natural planet of the earth and the only heavenly body visited by humans. With a diameter of 3475 kilometers and a mean distance of about 380,000 kilometers from earth, the Moon takes the same time (27.3 days) for one revolution around the earth and one rotation about its axis. This is the reason we always get to see only one face of the moon.

The Moon is also a royal planet and is considered the Queen in the hierarchy of Vedic Astrology. Chandra represents emotions, mind, mother, sensitivity, house, and household-related elements, including food and clothing, domestic comforts, sea, and all elements connected to the sea, milk, and the color associated with the Moon, white. She is cool, calm, and represents the north-eastern direction. Her metal is silver, and her gem is pearl.

Chandra is the fastest moving of the Navagrahas and takes about 2 ½ days in each Rashi. When Surya and Chandra are in the same Rashi or Zodiac Sign, it is Amavasya or the New Moon Day, which is also the first day of the dark fortnight. When the Sun and Moon are opposite each other, otherwise known as 180-degrees apart, then it is the Full Moon Day or Purnima, the bright fortnight's first day.

Chandra in Hindu Mythology - Another interesting story is that of the Moon or Chandra. Anasuya was the wife of Sage Atri, a great rishi of ancient times. Anusuya was known for her chastity. One day, the three prominent Hindu Gods, namely Vishnu, Shiva, and Brahma, tested her abstinence. They visited her in disguise and demanded that she feed them her breast milk.

Anusuya saw through the trick and changed the three gods into babies through her divine powers. It was now not a problem feeding the three babies the milk of her breast. The gods were pleased with her behavior and attitude and blessed her to have great sons. Through Vishnu's grace, Anusuya gave birth to Lord Dattatreya. Shiva's blessings resulted in the birth of Sage Durvasa. Lord Brahma's blessings resulted in the birth of the Moon God, Chandra.

Chandra was worshipped by all beings. He married the 27 daughters of Prajapati Daksha, and these 27 daughters became the 27 constellations or Nakshatras in the Zodiac. Interestingly, he preferred to remain with only one of his 27 wives and ignored the other 26 despite them pleading with him to spend time with them all equally.

The 26 daughters complained to their father, Prajapati Daksha, who warned his son-in-law of dire consequences if he is not fair to all his wives. Chandra did not heed his father-in-law's advice, who cursed him to fall ill. Every day, his glow faded, and there seemed to be no remedy for his illness. The gods were alarmed at the effects of life on earth if Chandra died.

So, they approached Daksha and requested him to adjust the curse so life on earth remains unaffected. Daksha agreed to change the curse only after Chandra promised to spend one day each with his 27 wives. With the curse modified, Chandra's would wane for 14 days and regain the glow during the next 14 days, which is the story of the moon's waxing and waning cycle.

Like the Suryavanshi, Chandravanshi was another powerful dynasty that ruled over India. The Chandravanshis believed they were direct descendants of the Moon God. The first king of the Chandravanshi Dynasty was Bharat, the legendary ruler, after whom India gets its Sanskrit name.

Important astrological facts about the moon - The sign in which the Moon is placed during your birth is called Janma Rashi. And the star constellation is your Nakshatra. Moon represents mind and emotion and signifies the mother relationship. Chandra's astrological nature is fickleness and changeability. The element governed by the Moon is water. The primary guna of Chandra is Sattva.

Astrologically, when the moon is waxing, its nature is beneficial. During the waning period, he has a malefic effect. The Moon's strength is felt when he is in the Fourth House, and his power is weak when in the 10th house. The Moon rules over the Zodiac sign, Cancer. Surya and Shukra are his friends, and he has no enemies. Positive elements connected with Chandra are receptivity, sympathy, good memory, and protectiveness. Negative elements relating to Chandra are touchiness, emotional instability, worry, moodiness, and smothering love.

Mangala, Guja, or Mars

Mangala Gruha, Mars is the first planet closest to earth's boundary in space. With a diameter of about 6700 kilometers, this fourth planet in our Solar System takes 687 days for one revolution around the Sign; the period of rotation on its axis is just over 24 hours. It has two natural satellites, namely Phobos and Deimos. The retrograde period of Mangala Gruha ranges between 60-80 days and happens once every 26 months.

Mangala or Guja in Hindu mythology – Once, Prajapati Daksha organized a grand yagna. All the gods and goddesses from all the three worlds were invited for this fabulous yagna. Out of earlier spite, Daksha deliberately left out Lord Shiva, who was also his son-in-law, from the invitation list.

Sati, Lord Shiva's wife, and Daksha's daughter were keen ongoing for the yagna even without an invitation. Lord Shive did not agree and warned her not to go to her father's house. But Sati ignored her husband's warnings and went to her father's abode.

On reaching the place where the yagna was being conducted, Sati was insulted by her insolent, arrogant father, who also made unpleasant remarks about Lord Shiva. Sati was so furious with Daksha she cursed the yagna and all the other invitees who did not find the courage to protest the powerful Daksha's unjust opinions. Eventually, Sati was consumed by the fire of her anger.

Shiva was livid when he heard of his wife's death. He tore a matt of hair from his head in a rage, and using his divine powers; he molded a thousand-limbed, ferocious monster named Virabhadra. Shiva ordered his son, Virabhadra, to destroy Daksha along with his supporter. Virabhadra completed this mission with resounding success, which pleased his lord and father.

Virabhadra and Shiva's other son, Lord Karthikeya, became brothers. This is the reason natives afflicted with the negative effects of Mangala Gruha pray to Lord Karthikeya for release.

Important astrological facts about Mars - Mars stands for strength and power and signifies siblings. His hierarchical position in Vedic Astrology is that of the army commander. Temperamentally, Mangala Gruha is rash, angry, and violent. He governs the fire element, and the primary quality is Tamas.

This Kshatriya's nature is malefic. His strength is felt the most when he is in the 10th House, and his power is at the weakest when he is in the fourth house. Mars rules over Aries (Mesha Rashi) and Scorpio (Vrischika Rashi). His friends are Surya, Chandra, and Guru. Only Shukra is his enemy. The Nakshatras Guja rules include Dhanishta, Mrigashirsha, and Chitra.

Guja is sometimes spelled as Kuja too. Mars is the commander in Vedic Astrology. He represents courage, energy, younger siblings, especially brothers (and hence is known as Bhatrukaraka or protector of brothers), police and armed forces, administrators, commanders, engineering, land, real estate, and other masculine kinds of activities. The metal of Mars is copper, the gem is coral, and its color is red. He represents the south direction. It takes Mars about 45 days to travel through one Zodiac Sign.

The positive emotions and behavioral attitudes connected to Mars are energy, courage, activity, originality, and initiative. The negative attitudes related to Mars are aggression, arrogance, selfishness, headstrong, and impulsive.

Buddha or Mercury

Being closest to the Sun, Mercury is a planet with a diameter of about 4800 kilometers. This planet takes 88 days to complete one revolution around the Sun and about 59 days for one rotation around its axis. It has no natural satellite of its own. Its retrograde period is about 20 to 24 days, which takes place once in approximately four months.

Buddha in Hindu Mythology - According to Hindu mythology, Buddha is Chandra, the Moon God's son. Chandra became a powerful divine being and conquered the three worlds, which led to him becoming highly arrogant. Chandra was one of the primary disciples of Guru, or Jupiter, the guru of the Devas. He was also a favorite of Jupiter's wife, Tara.

One day, when Jupiter was away, Tara and Chandra eloped. On returning home, when Jupiter found his bride missing, he realized what had happened. He sent multiple messages to Chandra to return his wife honorably to him. Chandra paid no heed to these requests, saying that Tara came of her own accord and would leave him only when she is satiated. Jupiter now turned to another of his disciples, Indra (the king of gods), for help. Indra sent an ultimatum to Chandra to return their guru's wife.

When Chandra refused to comply with his ultimatum too, Indra waged war against the Moon God. Venus (Jupiter's enemy), along with the Asuras, took Chandra's side while Lord Shiva and many devas fought alongside Indra in this war. The war went on for so long the wise sages feared the end of the world was near. Lord Brahma then ordered Chandra to return Tara to Jupiter. This time Chandra obliged, but not before making her pregnant with his child.

Jupiter forced Tara to abort Chandra's child. But the baby who was radiant and golden survived. Seeing the beauty of the baby, both the Moon and Jupiter claimed paternity. Both demanded that Tara declare the true name of the baby's father. Lord Brahma had to interfere again and asked Tara for the baby's father's name in private. At this point, Tara said that Chandra was the father of the child who was none other than Mercury or Buddha.

Important astrological facts about Mercury - known as the prince in Vedic Astrology, Mercury is a masculine planet. He represents intelligence, speech, maternal uncles, the medical profession, trade, computers and the internet, short journeys, astrology, knowledge of Shastras, journalism, mathematics, and printing and publishing. The gem of Mercury is emerald, and his metal is bronze. His color is green, and he represents the north direction. Mercury takes about a month to travel through one Zodiac sign.

Mercury is considered the god of speech, and relationship signifies maternal uncles. In the astrological hierarchy, Mercury is the Crown Prince, while his temperament is versatile and volatile. He governs the earth element and rules two Zodiac signs, namely Gemini (Mithunah) and Virgo (Kanya Rashi).

His nature is beneficial when combined with other favorable planets. Mercury's strength is when he is in the First House, and his weak position is the seventh house. His friends are Surya and Shukra, and his enemies are Chandra and Mangala. The Nakshatras that Mercury rules over are Ashlesha, Jayeshtha, and Revati.

Positive emotions connected with Mercury include alertness, brilliance, versatility, articulateness, and dexterity. Negative elements related to Mercury are nosiness, skepticism, restlessness, indecision, and criticalness.

Shukra, or Venus

Venus is the second farthest (after Mercury) planet from the sun and is the brightest heavenly body after the sun and moon. With a diameter of about 12000 kilometers, Venus or Shukra is the closest planet to the earth. It takes about 225 days for Venus to complete one revolution around the sun and about 243 days for one rotation around its axis. Venus has no natural satellite. Its retrograde period is about 40-43 days, which happens once every 19 months.

Shukra in Hindu Mythology - Shukra was the guru of the Daityas or Asuras. He knew the secret use of Sanjivini Vidya with which it was possible to revive the dead. He used this powerful knowledge to revive dead asuras. Also, Shukra was immensely learned and an astute Brahmin. He was handsome, intelligent, and sensuous. His father was Rishi Bhrigu, and his mother was Puloma.

One day, Venus was enjoying the beauty of nature as his father, Rishi Bhrigu, was deep in meditation nearby. Venus fell hopelessly in love with Apsara Viswachi, who had come to that spot. He followed her to heaven and created a small hut for her, living happily with Viswachi for many years until the effects of his good karma ended.

When his good karmas ended, Shukra's soul fell to the moon and then to the earth, where he was born as the son of a virtuous Brahmin. He led an austere life on Mount Meru for a long time until he met Viswachi again, who was cursed to be born as a female deer. Shukra fell in love with the deer, and through their union, a human child was born.

Then, the life of the Brahmin who held Shukra's soul ended. After his death, Shukra was reborn as the prince of Madra, which he ruled for many years. Like this, Shukra's soul was reborn multiple times on earth until his final birth was that of a son of a learned seer who lived on the banks of a river.

Meanwhile, Rishi Bhrigu opened his eyes after thousands of human years had passed and saw the worn-out body of his dead son, Shukra. In anger, he was about to curse Yama, the Lord of Death, who appeared before him and reminded him that Shukra's karma resulted in his multiple births and deaths. And that, right then, he was meditating on earth on the banks of a river.

The Lord of Death revived Shukra's body, who realized the truth behind his numerous births and deaths he had to undertake to cleanse himself of all karmic effects. Venus then meditated on Lord Shiva to achieve spiritual salvation. After thousands of years of meditation, Lord Shiva appeared to Shukra, taught him the Sanjivini Vidya, and gave him the boon of being the most auspicious planet among the nine planets.

Even today, marriages are performed only when Venus is rising in the sky. After that, Shukra had many wives and was blessed with several children too.

Important astrological facts about Venus - Venus is the guru of the demons or asuras and is known as Daitya guru. He represents sex life and sex organs, kidneys, spouse (and hence is called *Kalatrakaraka)*, dance, music and the arts, gems and jewels, bars, wines, gambling dens, fashion and cosmetics, and beauty products. The metal of Venus is silver, his color is white, his gem is diamond, and he represents the southeast direction. The planet Venus takes about a month to travel one Rashi, and like the Sun, takes one year to complete one round of the Zodiac.

Venus' significance is connected to desire and potency. He represents the spousal relationship. In the astrological hierarchy, Venus or Shukra is the Royal Advisor or Minister. His nature is accommodating, easy-going, and beneficial to everyone. Venus is related to the water element, and this primary Guna is Rajas, which stands for passion and imperiousness.

Venus' strength is at its peak when he is in the Fourth House, and he is the weakest in the 10th house. The Zodiac Signs he rules over are Taurus (Vrishabha Rashi) and Libra (Tula Rashi). His friends are Mercury (Buddha) and Shani (Saturn). His enemies are Surya and Chandra. He is neutral with Jupiter (Guru) and Mars (Mangala). Venus is the ruling planet of Bharani, Purva Phalguni, and Purvashada Nakshatras.

Venus relates to harmony, refinement, devotion, responsiveness, and affection. The negative emotions connected with Venus are indifference, laziness, superficial, flirtatious, and self-indulgence.

Guru, Brihaspathi, or Jupiter

Jupiter is the biggest planet in our Solar System, with a diameter of 142 800 kilometers. It takes 11.86 years to complete one revolution around the Sun and a little less than 10 hours to complete one rotation about its axis. Jupiter has 63 natural satellites. It retrogrades for about 110 days every approximately once every year.

Guru in Hindu Mythology - Guru or Brihaspati was one of Rishi Angiras' eight sons. His mother and Rishi Angiras' wife was Shraddha. After receiving the basic knowledge from his father, he left home in search of spiritual intelligence. He meditated for thousands of years to gain insight and wisdom. His relentless penances earned him a position of guru to the gods. His primary purpose was to protect and advance the interests of the devas (or gods) and thwart the designs and intentions of demons (or Asuras).

Once Shukra, the guru of the Asuras, went to the Himalayas to meditate and seek the power to conquer and destroy the devas from Lord Shiva. Indra, the devas' king, sent his daughter, Jayanthi, to deceive Shukra with her amorous charms and learn whatever Lord Shiva would teach him. She stayed with Shukra for many years until Lord Shiva appeared and taught them everything they wanted to learn.

When it was time to return to the devas' abode, Jayanthi had a change of heart. She revealed her true identity to Shukra and requested him to accept her as his wife. He agreed to her request but said he would be with her only for 10 years, and during this period, they would live alone.

Jupiter used this period of 10 years to disguise himself as Shukra so he could live with the Asuras and remove hatred and factionalism among them. Guru disguised as Shukra endeared himself to the Asuras. When the real Shukra returned, the Asuras were confused by two identical-looking gurus. They declared Jupiter (disguised as Shukra) to be their real guru. The real Shukra got angry and cursed them they would be destroyed soon.

Soon after, Jupiter changed into true form and left the Asuras' abode and went to the heavens. The demons now realized their mistake and rushed to their real guru and begged for his forgiveness. He relented and returned to be their guru. But his curse could not be taken back, and the Asuras became very weak to threaten the devas. In this way, Jupiter served his ardent followers, the devas.

Important astrological facts about Jupiter - Brihaspathi or Guru is known as the Devaguru or the guru to the gods. He represents spirituality, wisdom, temples, priests, research and science, teachers, lawyers and judges, and knowledge of astrology and other Shastras in the Sanatana Dharma. The metal of Jupiter is gold, the gem is the yellow sapphire, and the direction he represents is northeast. Guru takes one year to travel through one zodiac sign. Known as Putrakaraka, he is the protector of and connected with children and offspring.

Jupiter is related to fortune and knowledge. He represents the relationship with children, and like Shukra, holds a ministerial or advisory position in the Vedic astrological hierarchy. Jupiter's nature is benign, gentle, and mild. He governs the element, ether. His primary Guna is Sattva representing peace and serenity. His power is at its peak when he is in the first house and the weakest when he is in the seventh house.

Jupiter rules over Dhanush and Meena Rashis. His friends are Surya, Chandra, and Mangala, while his enemies are Buddha and Shukra. He has a neutral relationship with Shani. The three Nakshatras that Jupiter rules over include Punarvasu, Vishakha, and Purva Bhadra.

The positive emotions related to Jupiter are expansion, understanding, opportunity, enthusiasm, and optimism. The negative emotions connected with Jupiter are extravagance, indulgence, bigotry, smugness, and fanaticism.

Shani, or Saturn

With a 120 660 kilometers diameter, Saturn is the second-largest planet in our Solar System after Jupiter. Jupiter's most famous aspect concerns the complex ring system surrounding it. Saturn takes 29.5 years to complete one revolution around the Sun and a little less than 11 hours to complete one rotation about its axis. Saturn has 62 natural satellites, of which Titan is the largest satellite in our Solar System. Shani goes into retrograde once a year for about 135 days.

Shani in Hindu Mythology - Shani is represented as being very tall (with long limbs), with black skin, reddish-brown eyes, and an emaciated look. He is cruel in authoritative positions, and his gaze can terrify anyone. Shani is the son of Surya and his second wife, Chaaya. His brother is Lord Yama, the god of death and righteousness.

As soon as Shani was born, he looked at his father, Surya, who immediately got afflicted with vitiligo. Next, Shani looked at Arun, Surya's charioteer, who fell and broke his thighs. When he next gazed at the seven horses of Surya's chariot, their eyes turned to stone, and they became blind.

The Sun God tried various remedies to cure everyone. Although, nothing worked. Only when Saturn turned his gaze away did Surya's skin cleared, Arun's thighs were healed, and the seven horses got back their eyesight. Shani performed many years of penance at the holy city of Benares, where Lord Shiva appeared before him and gave him the position of a planet in the Zodiac.

Shani is the god of longevity, justice, death, and time. Even the king of gods, Indra, panics when Shani is nearby because thousands of Indras have been consumed by the power of time.

Important astrological facts about Shani - Shani is a servant in the hierarchy of Vedic Astrology. He represents sorrow, hard work, old men, servants, and other lower-level workers such as those in the iron and steel industry, drainage work, and municipality. Saturn placed in the right position on the Rashi chart can bestow prestige and power on the native. But Saturn in the wrong place can cause havoc and devastation in the life of the native.

Saturn's color is blue, his metal is iron, the gem is blue sapphire, and he represents the west direction. He is the slowest moving planet taking about 2 and ½ years in each Zodiac. Therefore, he takes 30 years to complete one round of the Zodiac. He is called Udyoga karaka because he is connected to professions.

He is connected to grief and misfortune. He represents subordinates or the workers at the lower order. The temperament of Saturn is cruel, harsh, and insensitivity. His nature is malefic. He is related to the Air element, and his primary Guna is Tamas, which stands for dullness and ignorance.

His strength is at its peak when Shani is in the seventh house, and he is weakest when he is in the first house. He rules over Makar and Kumbh Rashis. His friends are Shukra and Buddha, his enemies are Surya, Chandra, and Mangala, and he has a neutral relationship with Guru. The three Nakshatras he lords over include Pushya, Anuradha, and Uttara Bhadra.

The positive keywords related to Shani are experience, humility, patience, compassion, and wisdom. The negative emotions connected with Saturn are sorrow, challenges, delay, limitation, and disappointment.

Rahu, or the Dragon's Head, or the Lunar North Node and Ketu, or the Dragon's Tail, or the Lunar South Node

According to Vedic Astrology, Rahu and Ketu stand for the two points of intersection between the Sun and Moon's paths as they move around in the Zodiac. They are called the *south and north lunar nodes.* Eclipses occur when the Sun and the Moon are at one of these two places, which gave rise to the myth of the sun being swallowed.

Rahu and Ketu in Hindu Mythology - Rahu's father was Viprachitti, and his mother was Simhika. Simhika was the sister of Prahlad, the ardent Asura devotee of Lord Vishnu. Ketu is the dismembered body while Rahu is the head. Their story is part of the story of Amrit Manthan or the Churning of the Ocean.

The devas were losing their power, thanks to Sage Durvasa's curse. The king of devas, Indra, lost his kingdom to the Asuras. They went to Lord Brahma for help, who directed them to go to Lord Vishnu. Vishnu told Indra to approach the Asuras and ask for their help in churning the ocean so they could both get *amrita*, the nectar of immortality. Indra suggested to the Asuras that both could share the nectar and become immortal. The Asuras agreed to help in the churning of the ocean.

Mount Mandara was used as a rod, and Serpent Vasuki was used as a churning rope. Lord Vishnu took the form of a gigantic tortoise to hold up Mount Mandara and prevent it from slipping into the ocean. As the churning began, the Asuras on one side and the devas on the other, many things emerged from the ocean.

The poison, halahala, was the first thing that came up. It threatened to destroy both the devas and asuras. But Lord Shiva came to their rescue. He swallowed the poison and held it at this throat for eternity. Other important elements that emerged from the churning included the celestial horse, Ucchaishravas, Kamadhenu, the wish-fulfilling cow, Airavata, the white celestial elephant, Lakshmi, the goddess of wealth and prosperity, Apsaras, the beautiful dancers, the Kausthubha gem, and much more. Finally, the god of medicine, Dhanvantri, emerged holding a pot filled with amrita. The asuras snatched it and refused to share it with the devas.

At this time, Lord Vishnu was Mohini, an irresistible enchantress whom the asuras lusted after. They handed over the pot of nectar to Mohini and agreed to allow her to distribute the amrita as per her wishes. She asked the devas and asuras to sit in a line and distributed the nectar, beginning with the devas.

Rahu realized something was amiss. He disguised himself as a deva and sat between Surya and Chandra, who recognized him immediately. Vishnu, in the form of Mohini, threw his discus and severed Rahu's head. But Rahu managed to drink one tiny drop of the nectar, making himself immortal just in time.

Therefore, although his head and body were separate, both the parts remained immortal. The head was called Rahu, and the headless body got the name Ketu. These two are continually chasing the Sun and Moon gods because they were the ones who sneaked to Mohini about his presence. When they catch him, they swallow the sun and moon, causing solar and lunar eclipses. But, as Rahu and Ketu cannot hold him for long, the sun and moon come out intact because they have also had their share of the nectar of immortality.

Important astrological facts about Rahu - This shadow planet represents foreign countries, foreigners, international travel, smoke, engineering and technical industries and trade, drinking, gambling, grandparents. He also represents the underworld and the dark, shadow life in a society. Rahu's color is black, he represents a mixed metal, and his gem is Gomedh or hessonite garnet. Rahu takes about 1 and ½ years to travel a Zodiac sign, and therefore, takes 18 years to complete one round of the Zodiac.

Rahu represents maternal grandparents and is known for spiritual knowledge. He represents the air element. Rahu lords over Ardra, Swati, and Shatabhisha Nakshatras. Rahu's positive keywords are independence, originality, inspiration, insight, and imagination and negative keywords are deception, confusion, addiction, illusion, and neurosis.

Important Astrological Facts About Ketu - Representing grandparents, spiritual inclinations, technical and electronics trades, superstitions, Ketu, like Rahu, takes about 1 and ½ years to complete one Zodiac. Ketu represents paternal grandparents and stands for moksha or ultimate liberation. The temperaments of both Rahu and Ketu are unpredictable and erratic. Ketu represents the fire element. The primary quality of Rahu and Ketu is Tamas. Their natures of both planets are malefic.

Ketu rules over Ashwini, Magha, and Moola Nakshatra. Rahu and Ketu's friends are Shukra, Mangala, and Shani, their enemies are Surya and Chandra, and they have a neutral relationship with Guru and Buddha. Ketu's positive keywords are self-sacrifice, idealism, spirituality, compassion, and intuition, and negative keywords are eccentricity, fanaticism, amorality, violence, and impulsiveness.

Each of the nine planets has different effects, good and bad, on the native's life depending on their placements in the various Rashis. Interestingly, the effects on a person's life could be diagrammatically opposite to that of another individual. Seven out of the nine (Rahu and Ketu are left out) planets also rule the seven days of the week as under:

- Surya rules Sunday.
- Chandra rules Monday.
- Mangala rules Tuesday.
- Buddha rules Wednesday.
- Guru rules Thursday.
- Shukra rules Friday.
- Shani rules Saturday.

Now that you have a good idea about the nine planets and their significance, it is time to see how they influence our daily lives.

Chapter 3: Planetary Influences on Daily Life

Understanding planetary influences on our daily life requires us to know more about the relationships shared by the nine planets, their positions on the Zodiac, and the direct and special aspects of each planet. Let us know more about these and other elements in Vedic Astrology.

Five-Fold Relationship

Called *Panchada Maitri* in Sanskrit, planetary relationships are complex. It is important to know that the power of a planet depends on his own position and the relative position with other planets. Planets are powerful if they are in any one of these positions:

- In the house of the sign(s) of their exaltation.
- In their own house.
- In the house of their friends.

Planets are weak when, in one of these positions:

- In the house of their enemies.
- In the house of the sign(s) of their debilitation.

The strength of the planets is neutral in the house of neutral signs.

When two planets have a relationship-based influence over each other, then the effects on the concerned natives depend on the quality of these interplanetary relations. The planets have different relationships and friends, including a great (or fast) friend (ati mitra), a good friend (mitra), neutral (sama), bitter enemies (ati shatru), and enemies or inimical (shatru). This concept is called *Panchada Maitri,* which is of four types of relationships, including:

Parivartana or Exchange Relationship - This two-way exchange is the most powerful of all the four types. It is based on mutual sign ownership. This happens when two planets are in two houses owned by each other.

Aspect or Drishti Relationship - This is a one-way exchange wherein one planet is in the house owned by another planet. Also, the house is aspected significantly. If the aspect is almost total, then this relationship is also very powerful.

Posited in the Same Sign - When two planets are posited together in the same sign, then too, the exchange is powerful.

Mutual Aspect - This happens when two planets mutually aspect each other. If this happens at near-total levels, then too, the exchange can be powerful.

The interplanetary relationships of each planet are also determined by their Tatkalik (temporal) and Naisargik (natural or permanent) friendships. Permanent friendships and relationships depend on the planets' natural status, whereas temporal relationships depend on the position of the planets in individual horoscopes.

The third relationship is the neutral type (or Sama), wherein the planets are neither friends nor enemies but are neutral towards each other. Both enjoy equal status. The relation is always seen from the perspective of the planet under consideration. For example, suppose you want to see the link of Surya with other planets. There, its tie is judged from Surya's viewpoint and is independent of the other planet's attitudes toward Surya.

Chart analysis is rarely done using Naisargika relationships. It is only used to compute Panchadha Maitree. The temporal links are the ones used for chart analysis. So, if Chandra is not hostile towards any planet in its Naisargika relationships, then it only means that in the Panchada Maitri Scheme, he will never be a sworn enemy of other planets. Although, if there is hostility from Chandra's perspective in the Tatkalika relationships, then it can be hostile to another planet in the Panchada Maitri Scheme.

Naisargika friendship works like this. Satyacharya's rule governs Naisargika relationships. From the Mooltrikona sign of any graha, the lords of the 2nd, 4th, 5th, 8th, 9th, 12th, and the lord of the exaltation sign are his friends. The lords of the other houses, namely the 3rd, 6th, 7th, 10th, and 11th, are hostile towards this planet. But the lord of the planet's exaltation sign will also be a friend, even if he is in one of the inimical houses. The lords who own both are neutral. If a planet becomes a friend and enemy because of owning two houses, then it is considered a neutral planet.

Naisargika friendships are permanent and are not influenced by the position of the planets in the elliptical. The planets are friendly or hostile due to their inherent characteristics. The rays of the planet will be intensified by the rays of mitra planets and counteracted or weakened by enemy or shatru planets.

Tatkalik relationships work like this. The planets in the second, third, fourth, eleventh, or twelfth houses from each planet become temporary mitra or friends, and the planets in the other houses are temporarily inimical.

Panchada Maitri is arrived at by combining Naisargika and Tatkalika friends:

• If two planets are friendly in both Naisargika and Tatkalika perspectives, then they are extremely friendly in the native's horoscope; permanent friend + temporary friend = best friend.

• If they are friendly through one view and have a neutral relationship through the other, then the result is friendly; permanent friend + temporary enemy = neutral.

• If enmity combines with affinity, then the result is equality; permanent enemy + temporary friend = neutral

• Enmity combining with neutral results in enmity.

• If there is enmity from both accounts, then the result is extreme enmity; permanent enemy + temporary enemy = bitter enemy.

The Mooltrikona positions of the seven planets are:

• Surya in Simha Rashi up to 20-degrees.

• Chandra in Vrishabha Rashi up to 27-degrees.

• Mangala in Mesha Rashi up to 12-degrees.

• Buddha in Kanya Rashi up to 20-degrees.

• Guru in Dhanush Rashi up to 10-degrees.

• Shukra in Tula Rashi up to 15-degrees.

• Shani in Kumbha Rashi up to 20-degrees.

Using these rules, the friendship-enmity relationships of Naisargika friendship for each of the seven planets is:

Surya - Surya represents good fortune, soul, career, father-figure, and authority. The aspects of the Sun are not malefic in nature. However, he can cause feelings of cruelty, egotistical acts, and selfishness.

The Mooltrikona is Simha Rashi (Leo). The 4th, 2nd, 12th, 5th, 9th, and 8th houses hold Mangala, Buddha, Chandra, Guru, Mangala, and Guru, respectively. Surya's sign of exaltation is Mangala. Therefore, Mangala, Buddha, Chandra, and Guru are his friends.

The lords of the 3rd, 6th, 7th, 10th, and 11th in relation to Surya are Shukra, Shani, Shani, Shukra, and Buddha. Shani and Shukra are Surya's enemies. Buddha holds a house of a friend and that of an enemy for Surya. Buddha has a neutral relationship with Surya.

Chandra - Chandra or the Moon desires family, mind, and the mind's obsessions and home. The Mooltrikona of Chandra in Vrishabha Rashi (Taurus). The 4th, 2nd, 12th, 5th, 9th, and 8th houses hold Surya, Buddha, Mangala, Buddha, Shani, Guru, who are Chandra's friends. Chandra's exaltation sign is Shukra, who is also Chandra's friend, regardless of the house he occupies.

The lords of the 3rd, 6th, 7th, 10th, and 11th, in relation to Chandra's Mooltrikona, are Chandra, Shukra, Mangala, Shani, and Guru, respectively. Shukra has an inimical position with respect to Chandra and his sign of exaltation. Shukra's relationship with Chandra is neutral. Similarly, Mangala, Shani, and Guru will have a neutral exchange with Chandra because they share a friendly and an inimical relationship.

Buddha - Buddha or Mercury represents speech, intellect, learning and understanding, communication, and profession. The Mooltrikona of Buddha is Kanya Rashi (Virgo). The lords of the 4th, 2nd, 12th, 5th, 9th, and 8th houses in accord to Buddha's position are Guru, Shukra, Surya, Shani, Shukra, and Mangala, resulting in a friendly relationship with Buddha (Mercury). The sign of exaltation is Mercury himself.

The lords of the 3rd, 6th, 7th, 10th, and 11th houses are Mangala, Shani, Guru, Buddha, and Chandra. Using the Panchada Maitri rules, Mangala and Shani have a neutral relationship with Buddha because they are lords of friendly and an inimical house in accord to Buddha's Mooltrikona position.

Shukra - Shukra or Venus represents love, sensuality, peace, sex, materialistic comforts, and love-based relationships. The Mooltrikona of Shukra is Tula Rashi (Libra). The lords of the 4th, 2nd, 12th, 5th, 9th, and 8th houses in relationship to Shukra are Shani, Mangala, Buddha, Shani, Buddha, and Shukra, respectively, giving them a friendly relationship. The sign of exaltation of Shukra is Guru.

The lords of the 3rd, 6th, 7th, 10th, and 11th houses are Guru, Guru, Mangala, Chandra, and Surya, subsequently, giving them an inimical relationship with Shukra. Guru and Mangala will have a neutral link with Shukra as each occupies a friendly and an inimical house.

Mangala - Mangala or Mars desires and represents conflicts, ambition, power, and property. The Mooltrikona of Mangala (Mars) is Mesha Rashi (Aries). The lords of the 4th, 2nd, 12th, 5th, 9th, and 8th houses in relationship to Mars are Chandra, Shukra, Guru, Surya, Guru, and Mangala, respectively, giving them a friendly link with Mars. The sign of exaltation of Mangala is Shani.

The lords of the 3rd, 6th, 7th, 10th, and 11th houses regarding Mars' Mooltrikona position are Buddha, Buddha, Shukra, Shani, and Shani, then giving them a relationship of enmity. Shukra and Shani will have a neutral relationship with Mangala because they occupy a friendly and an inimical position.

Guru - Guru represents knowledge, spirituality, good fortune, values, and religion. The Mooltrikona of Guru (Jupiter) is Dhanush Rashi (Sagittarius). The lords of the 4th, 2nd, 12th, 5th, 9th, and 8th houses in relationship to Guru's Mooltrikona position are Guru,

Shani, Mangala, Mangala, Surya, and Chandra, resulting in a friendly relationship. Guru's sign of exaltation is Chandra.

The lords of the 3rd, 6th, 7th, 10th, and 11th houses regarding Guru are Shani, Shukra, Buddha, Buddha, and Shukra, resulting in an inimical relationship. Shani has a neutral relationship with Guru.

Shani - Shani represents suffering, hard work, poverty, illness, and finality. The Mooltrikona of Shani (Saturn) is Kumbh Rashi (Aquarius). he lords of the 4th, 2nd, 12th, 5th, 9th, and 8th houses in relationship to Shani are Shukra, Guru, Shani, Buddha, and Shukra, respectively, giving them a friendly relation. The sign of exaltation of Shani is Shukra.

The lords of the 3rd, 6th, 7th, 10th, and 11th houses regarding Shani are Mangala, Chandra, Surya, Mangala, and Guru, giving them a relationship of enmity with Shani. Guru shares a neutral relationship with Shani because he occupies a friendly and an inimical position.

Natural Friends and Enemies of Rahu and Ketu

Rahu stands for manipulation, enjoyment, and ambition. He can cause cheating, shocks, and losses for natives. Rahu's Mooltrikona is Mithuna Rashi (Gemini). So, his friends should be the lords of Cancer, Virgo, Libra, Capricorn, Aquarius, and Taurus. His enemies would be the lords of Leo, Scorpio, Sagittarius, Pisces, and Aries.

Rahu's exaltation sign is Taurus, which is the 12th house from his Mooltrikona, already a friendly position. According to the Panchada Maitri rules, Chandra, Shukra, and Rahu are natural friends of Rahu, whereas Surya, Mangala, and Guru are his natural enemies. Buddha is neutral.

Ketu has no aspects because he represents no desires. Ketu's Mooltrikona is Dhanush Rashi (Sagittarius). So, Ketu's friendly signs are Capricorn, Pisces, Aries, Leo, Cancer, and Scorpio. His enemy signs are Aquarius, Taurus, Gemini, Virgo, and Libra. Ketu's exaltation sign is Scorpio, which is already in a friendly relationship occupying the 12th house.

Ketu's friends are Surya, Chandra, and Mangala, while his natural enemies are Shukra and Buddha. Shani and Guru have a neutral relationship with Ketu.

The following list summarizes the friends, enemies, and neutral relationships of the nine planets:

Surya - Surya's (or the Sun) friends are Moon (Chandra), Mars (Mangala), and Jupiter (Guru). His enemies are Shukra (Venus), Shani (Saturn), and Rahu. Neutral planets are Buddha and Ketu.

Chandra - Chandra's (or the Moon) friends are Surya and Shukra. His enemies are none, and he has a neutral relationship with Mangala, Guru, Shukra, Shani, Rahu, and Ketu.

Buddha - Buddha's (or Mercury) friends are Surya and Shukra. His enemies are Chandra and Ketu. He has neutral relationships with Mangala, Guru, Shani, and Rahu.

Shukra - Shukra (or Venus) friends are Buddha, Shani, and Rahu. His enemies are Surya and Chandra. He has a neutral relationship with Mangala, Guru, and Ketu.

Mangala - Mangala's (Mars) friends are Surya, Chandra, and Guru. His enemy is Buddha. And he is neutral with Shukra, Shani, Rahu, and Ketu.

Guru - Guru's (or Jupiter) friends are Surya, Chandra, and Mangala. His enemies are Buddha, Shukra, and Rahu. Guru has a neutral relationship with Shani and Ketu.

Shani - Shani's (or Saturn) friends are Buddha, Shukra, and Rahu. His enemies are Surya, Chandra, Mangala, and Rahu. He has a neutral relationship with Buddha and Guru.

Rahu - Rahu's friends are Shukra and Shani. His enemies are Surya, Chandra, and Mangala. He has a neutral relationship with Buddha, Guru, and Ketu.

Ketu - Ketu's friends are Surya and Mangala. His enemies are Shukra and Shani. He has a neutral relationship with Buddha, Guru, Chandra, and Rahu.

Reciprocal and Non-Reciprocal Friendships, Enmity, and Relationships

Surya is friendly with Mangala, Guru, and Chandra. These three planets, in turn, reciprocate the friendship towards Surya. Surya's enemies are Shani and Shukra, and they, in turn, are Surya's enemies. These relationships are termed as reciprocal.

Now, let us take another example. Surya is tolerant or neutral towards Buddha. Interestingly, Buddha likes Surya and considers him to be a friend. This kind of relationship is termed as non-reciprocal. The non-reciprocal types of relationships are interesting ones and give us a lot of insight and information into life.

Non-reciprocal friendships are ambiguously explained in the various texts of Vedic Astrology. But the most important component to support friendships and enmity of a planet with other planets is the planet itself, the one posited in the Mooltrikona, which is being considered. Parashara's text clearly states that the feelings of that planet towards other planets should be the determining factor of its relationships with other planets.

Logically too, this interpretation makes a lot of sense. Let us look at an example of the non-reciprocal relationship between Surya and Buddha to understand this interpretation. Now, Surya or the Sun represents authority and the soul or the consciousness. Buddha represents free speech and intellect. There is a complex but inevitable relationship between authority, consciousness, free speech, and intellect.

Mercury, the representative of free speech and intellect, likes Surya because both representative elements, namely intellect and free speech, need the support and help of authority/government and the illumination of the consciousness or the soul. So, Buddha or Mercury likes Surya.

Now, let us look at Surya and Buddha's relationship from Surya's (the representative of authority) perspective. The government or people in authority are not fond of those using free speech or free thinkers. Freethinkers and supporters of free speech are tolerated but not hated. So, Surya is neutral towards, in other words, he "tolerates" Buddha. This interpretation works for nearly all non-reciprocal relationships. Here are a few more examples which are useful tools to remember relationships between planets.

Mercury's non-reciprocal relationships - Next, let us look at Buddha in a little more detail. Mercury likes Venus (Shukra), who reciprocates this friendship happily, which is a reciprocal relationship. Mercury tolerates Mars (Mangala). But Mangala hates Buddha. Again, it is easy to understand logically. Mars represents the military who hate free thinkers, represented by Mercury. Freethinkers, on the other hand, put up or tolerate the military and the police because free thinkers not only understand the perspectives of the police and military, but they also need them for protection and security.

Another non-reciprocal relationship of Mercury is with Saturn. Mercury is neutral (or tolerates) Shani, whereas Shani likes Mercury. Shani is antagonistic towards authority, which can turn off Mercury. Although Mercury is lighthearted, he can tolerate Shani but cannot be on friendly terms.

Mercury and Jupiter (Guru) also share a non-reciprocal relationship. While Jupiter hates Mercury, Mercury is tolerant towards Jupiter. Jupiter stands for religion and dogma. Freethinkers and free speech supporters are continuously finding ways to embarrass religious dogmas even if they are open to (or neutral towards) religion. At this juncture, it might make sense to recall Shukra's mythology (born of Chandra and Tara, wife of Guru), who is the bastard son of Jupiter. So, while Mercury embarrasses his stepfather, Jupiter hates his bastard son.

Venus' non-reciprocal relationships - Venus is a friend of Saturn and Mercury, and both these planets reciprocate the relationship. In Vedic Astrology, the friendship between Venus (Shukra) and Saturn (Shani) is of legendary quality and is believed to be one of the strongest relationships, comparable to the relationship between Mars (Mangala) and Sun (Surya).

Venus' arch enemies are the Sun and Moon, and it is easy to understand this, considering that Venus represents creativity and the arts, both of which are usually anti-authoritarian. The Sun also dislikes Venus. But the Moon tolerates Venus' hatred.

Venus and Mars are neutral towards each other, representing the natural male-female dynamics of the universe. After all, men and women cannot live without each other, and yet find it difficult to live happily with each other, and end up tolerating one another.

Venus has a neutral relationship with Jupiter, although Jupiter does not like Venus. Again, this neutrality versus dislike non-reciprocal relationship is easy to understand. Venus stands for love, peace, and sensuality and can easily see value in religion and philosophy represented by Jupiter. While numerous forms of art and artists have been supported by religion, a lot more art-related works and people have been censored by religion.

While most artists tolerate religion, religion dislikes nearly all artists and artworks not conformed to or aligned with its beliefs and dogmas. Religion uses censorship to demonstrate its dislike for art.

Mars' Non-Reciprocal Relationships - Mars and Jupiter have a reciprocal friendly relationship. Mars representing energy and passion, knows he needs guidance represented by Jupiter. And Mars represents the enforcement agencies like the police and military, and Jupiter represents the morality-based order of enforcement, resulting in mutual, reciprocal friendship.

Mars and Saturn share a non-reciprocal relationship. Shani, representing anti-authority, hates the commanding and enforcement tendency of Mars. But Mars appreciates the practicality and tenacity of Saturn or Shani, and tolerates him.

Jupiter's Non-Reciprocal Relationship - Jupiter and Saturn tolerate each other because religion and morality (Jupiter) are inextricably intertwined with finality, represented by Saturn. Therefore, both tolerate each other even if they are totally opposite of each other.

Interestingly, no one really dislikes Jupiter, including the planets whom he ill-treats (Venus and Mercury). This likable aspect of Jupiter is based on all positive elements, including good deeds. He is a very sensitive lord and deals sensitively with others, even when doing something bad. Hence, no planet really dislikes Jupiter.

Chapter 4: House Systems and Characteristics of Bhava

Understanding the systems of houses in Vedic Astrology is the start of the basics of this fascinating subject. The Zodiac elliptical is 360-degrees, which is divided into 12 equal divisions of 30 degrees each. Each division is called a *Zodiac sign* or *house*. This 12-house system starts from Aries and finishes at Pisces.

Each of the 12 signs has one ruler (a planet), and planets rule two signs (dual ownership). An important element about dual ownership is that when a planet rules over two signs, then one of them is more important than the other. This concept is relative and is regardless of the planet and the signs it rules over. The more important sign becomes the Mooltrikona sign for that planet.

In Vedic Astrology, a planet is a heavenly body being considered in the Zodiac elliptic. The word "planet" should not be confused with its astronomical meaning. Planets need not be the same as defined by Physics and Astronomy. For example, Sun and Moon are taken as planets, even if Physics calls Sun a star and Moon a natural satellite.

To reiterate an earlier lesson, the nine primary planets of Vedic Astrology are Sun (Surya), Moon (Chandra), Mars (Mangala), Jupiter (Guru), Saturn (Shani), Mercury (Buddha), Venus (Shukra), and Rahu and Ketu. These last two are called *Shadow Planets.* Rahu and Ketu are not physical entities. They are imaginary points on the Zodiacal elliptic, where the axis of the Sun and Moon overlap, relative to earth. It is important to know that Rahu and Ketu are mathematical calculations and not physical entities like the other seven heavenly bodies collectively known as planets. The effects of Rahu and Ketu are so powerful on horoscopes that the ancient seers thought it important to give them planet status. They are always at 180-degrees from each other.

Rahu and Ketu do not rule over any signs considering they are not physical entities. But they are co-rulers of certain signs. Also, these two astrological elements are called shadow planets because they mirror the effects of the planets they are close to or the signs they occupy temporarily.

The 12 Houses or Bhavas

The 12 houses and their ruling planets are:

1. Aries (Mesha Rashi) -ruled by Mars (Mangala); the Mool Trikona (MK) sign for Mars in Aries

2. Taurus (Vrishabha Rashi) - ruled by Venus (Shukra)

3. Gemini (Mithuna Rashi) - ruled by Mercury (Buddha)

4. Cancer (Karkata Rashi) - ruled by Moon (Chandra)

5. Leo (Simha Rashi) - ruled by Sun (Surya)

6. Virgo (Kanya Rashi) - ruled by Buddha and Rahu - MK sign of Buddha

7. Libra (Tula Rashi - ruled by Shukra (MK sign)

8. Scorpio (Vrishchika Rashi) - ruled by Mars (Mangala) and Ketu

9. Sagittarius (Dhanush Rashi) - ruled by Jupiter (Guru) - MK sign

10. Capricorn (Makar Rashi) -ruled by Saturn

11. Aquarius (Kumbh Rashi) - ruled by Saturn (MK sign) and Rahu (co-ruler)

12. Pisces (Meena Rashi) - ruled by Jupiter

The term "Bhava" in Sanskrit means state or condition. In Jyotishya, Bhava is used to denote a fixed division in the Zodiac. It corresponds to the term 'house' used in Western Astrology. A natal or birth chart in Vedic Astrology is called *bhavachakra*, where chakra means "wheel" or "circle".

All charts have the same twelve bhavas or houses measuring 30 degrees each. The difference between individual charts is which house is taken as the first house, second house, and so forth until the 12 house. The Lagna or the Ascendant Sign determines the first house. The Lagna is the sign rising in the east at the time of the native's birth. The Lagna house is the first house for that person, and the others follow counter-clockwise, in the same sequence as the Zodiac elliptic.

The twelve houses rule over numerous aspects of an individual's life. Elements that each house rules over are given below. But it is important to remember that this list is not exhaustive.

The First House - Or the Lagna bhava, primarily represents the native's personality. It controls or rules over these aspects of a native's life, personality, behavior, physical appearances, etc.:

- The personality of the individual

- The head and the hair on the head

- Skull, skin, brain

- General health status including immunity and vitality

- Overall success, happiness, and wellbeing

- General physical characteristics of the native

- General mental characteristics

- Place of birth

- Thoughts and the working of the mind

- Power and status in society and family

- Starting of events and happenings

The Second House - Mainly stands for wealth and is called the *house of Dhana bhava* (wealth in Sanskrit). It represents and governs these aspects of the concerned native:

- It is the primary house of wealth, including assets like savings, property, retirement accounts, etc.

- Material possessions like clothes, jewelry, and household articles.

- Family of the native

- Face, mouth, and the tongue area and speech

- Left eye for the female and right eye for the male native along with general eyesight

- It is the place of death or the house with the potential to kill the native

- Basic education (until 3rd grade)

The Third House - Called *Parakrama* (courage) or *bhratru* (brothers), reflects the valor and courage of the native. It represents and governs these aspects of an individual's life:

- Siblings of the native, especially the younger siblings

- Neighbors and other people around the native

- Courage and valor of the person

- Throat and neck area including communication and speech

- Ears and hearing

- Communication aspects such as journalism, media, IT, internet, phones, computers, writing books and articles, and handwriting

- Short distance travel and short-term goals including hobbies

- Activities connected with the hands and arms

- Enthusiasm for work

- Libido and sexual prowess

The Fourth House - Called *"Suhdra"* of *"sukha"*, reflects the mother relationship. rules over these aspects of a person's life:

- Mother

- Motherland

- Vehicles

- Fixed property such as land, houses, and other forms of real estate, including agricultural land

- Emotions and happiness

- Luxuries and comfort (or the lack of it)

- Place of residence

- Chest, lungs, heart, the upper part of the spine,

- Private life and feelings

- Peace of mind

- High school level education, up to Grade 12

The Fifth House - Demonstrates children of the native. It governs these elements in an individual's life:

- Creativity

- Children, an element of our creation,

- Imagination

- Romance and love-based emotions

- Memory and fluid intelligence

- Speculation including playing on the stock markets and gambling

- Competition

- Good karma of the past lives

- House of wealth

- Diplomacy

- Royal or powerful positions and fame

- College or higher education

- Stomach, the lower part of the heart, liver, kidneys, spleen, and lower back

The Sixth House - Ripu/Roga, which translates to *disease* in Sanskrit, showcases enmity and diseases of the native. rules over these aspects of our life:

- Anything that opposes us, including our rivals and enemies and people who compete with us

- Short term sickness, diseases, surgeries, injuries,

- Debt, litigation, and courts

- Breaking of relationships

- The day-to-day grind of work

- Agony and physical pain

- Service and servants

- Theft and thieves

- Animals

- Fire

- Hygiene and medicine

- Critical thoughts about ourselves and about others

• Pancreas, small intestine, lower back, kidneys, urinary bladder

• Pregnancy, only for female natives

The Seventh House - Kama reflects the sexual energy of the native. It determines these aspects of our lives:

• Relationships including how we interact with and relate to people

• Legal contracts and business contracts

• Partnerships including marriage, spouse, and married life

• Foreign places

• Foreign residence or home far from birth town

• External sexual organs, sexual habits, and sexuality

• Large intestine and anal area

• "Maraka" place or the place with the potential to end the life of the native concerned

The Eight House - *Mrityu* (or death) governs these aspects:

• Transformations

• Obstacles and turnarounds in life

• Sudden events like tragic and serious accidents and injuries

• Deep emotions and turmoil,

• Death and death like events

• Degenerate and addictive habits like alcoholism, smoking, taking drugs, etc.

• Hidden things including interest in the occult and metaphysics

• Deep research or deep-dive analysis of any area seeking to understand intriguing things

- Regenerate and spiritual habits including detachment from materialism, success

- Loans or unearned money like legacies and inheritances

- Change of lifestyle, home, job, or other activity

- Mental anguish and despair, including hopelessness

- Internal sexual organs, anal area, testes, only for males

- Chronic and incurable diseases including terminal sickness

The Ninth House - Bhagya, is the house of luck and fortune. It determines these factors of our life:

- Father, guru, boss or employer

- Destiny and luck

- Higher education, research

- Temples

- Crystallized intelligence relating to one's beliefs, religion, spirituality, meditation, etc.

- Long distance and foreign travel

- Good deeds of previous lives

- Divine blessings help

- House of wealth

- Abstract thinking

- Crossing intellectual boundaries into new cultures, beliefs, and religion

- Foreign residence

- Publishing

- Import-export

- Hips, thighs, and tailbone area

The Tenth House - Karma rules over these factors of our life:

- Career and job
- Status in public life
- External manifestation of our work
- Fame, popularity, prestige, and honor
- Rise in life
- Karma (our actions)
- Energy levels and image at the workplace
- Recognition from Government
- Powerful positions like politicians, CEOs, directors of institutes
- Management-related positions
- Knees and middle parts of the legs

The 11th House - Aya, lords over these aspects of our life:

- Gains and income
- Rewards from workplace and job including promotions
- Wealth house
- Long term desires, goals, and their fulfillment
- Elder siblings
- Ears and hearing
- Social circle, friends, and social interaction
- Recovery from diseases and illnesses
- Ankles and lower feet area
- Prize and/or recognition from authorities, including the government

The **12th House** - Vyaya, determines these aspects of a native's life:

- Loss and expenses
- Letting go
- Isolation, imprisonment
- Loss of movement including being hospitalized
- Loss of freedom like being imprisonment
- Deep emotions such as grief and sadness
- Hidden life including sleep, sexual activity, hidden weaknesses, strengths, enemies
- Foreign residence and far-off isolated places
- Dreams, intuition, psychic powers
- Meditation and spirituality
- Lack of materialism
- Moksha
- Long-distance travel and settlement
- Feet, left eye for males, right eye for females
- Undiagnosable diseases
- Sleep-related problems like insomnia, somnambulism, etc.

Interesting Points about the Various Houses

The third and eighth houses or bhavas represent "Jeeva Shakti" or life force, and the 12th house deals with death, ending, or loss. Therefore, the 12th house to any bhava represents the loss or end of that bhava.

The 2nd and 7th houses are 12th houses from 3rd and 8th respectively, making them "Maraka" or killer houses. In the same way, the ninth house represents destiny and good fortune. The 12th from the 9th house is the 8th bhava, which is bad fortune and destruction.

Generally, houses 1, 5, and 9 are considered to give good things, including wealth, good health, good fortune, wisdom, education, etc. although there are other caveats to be considered for an accurate understanding of a person's birth chart. These three bhavas or houses are collectively called the "trikona" or triangle or the trine. Guru and Chandra are good when they are in the trine.

Houses 1, 4, 7, and 10 are called *Kendra* or the *Center* because they rule over most of our day-to-day life elements. These four houses are very important, and planets occupying these houses significantly influence the life of a native. The tenth house is the strongest and can overcome even the ascendant.

Houses 6, 8, and 12 are called bad houses or "dusthanas" as they stand for elements and things that oppose our happiness and bring grief, pain, losses, and agony.

A fourth category of bhavas is called *Upachaya*, remedial, or growth houses. In these houses, including the 3rd, 6th, 10th, and 11th, the malefic planets have a tendency to improve. This category is called "*increasing houses*," which means planets tend to give more over time. Shani and Mangala do well here and empower the natives with energy and strength to overcome obstacles. Malefic planets do well in the 11th house.

Apachaya or the houses of decrease include 1st, 2nd, 4th, 7th, and 8th bhavas, where the planets lose their strength. Malefics do not do well in these houses.

Another category called *succedent* or *fixed* includes the 2nd, 5th, 8th, and 11th bhavas. They reflect the accumulation and maintenance of our resources.

The cadent category includes the 3rd, 6th, 9th, and 12th houses. They give flexibility, intelligence, and adaptability. But they can get unstable and uncertain, leading to mental and nervous issues.

Further, the 12 houses or bhavas are divided into four categories based on the four important goals of human life as follows:

1. **Dharma** - 1st, 5th, and 9th houses stand for *dharma*, which reflects our need to find the path and purpose of our lives.

2. **Artha** - the 2nd, 6th, and 10th houses represent the *artha* or wealth creation. These three bhavas reflect the human need to acquire the necessary materialistic abilities and resources to achieve our purpose.

3. **Kama** - the 3rd, 7th, and 11th houses stand for pleasure and enjoyment, a basic need of human life.

4. **Moksha** - the 4th, 8th, and 12th houses represent our desire for enlightenment and freedom from the struggle of the limitless cycles of birth and death.

Understanding Bhavatah Bhava

Bhavatah bhava means the future bhava from a particular house. Bhavat translates to "future." Bhavatah Bhava applies to the house that is the same number as the house counted from the Lagna bhava. Bhavatah Bhava is like a house or bhava being born again in the future. Bhavatah bhava is an important technique used in Vedic Astrology to make accurate predictions. Let us look at examples to better understand the concept of Bhavatah Bhava:

• The 3rd bhava or house because it is the 2nd house of the 2nd house. Counted in the same way (considering houses are counted counterclockwise in a circular path), the 3rd house is also the bhavatah bhava of the 8th house (because it is the 8th from the 8th house). In the same way, the following bhavatah bhavas can be arrived at:

• The 11th house is the bhavatah bhava for the 12th (12th from 12th) and the 6th (6th from the 6th house).

- The 5th house is the bhavatah bhava for the 3rd house and the 9th house.

- The 9th house is the bhavatah bhava for the 11th and the 5th houses.

- The 7th house is the bhavatah bhava for 4th and the 10th houses.

- The 1st house is the bhavatah bhava for the 7th house.

In this concept, the bhavatah bhava concept reflects sharing similar indications. For example, the 5th house stands for intellect and reflects the wisdom and deep learning. The 9th house, which is the bhavatah bhava for the 5th house, also supports these attributes as it stands for higher education or university education.

Similarly, the 5th bhava supports and aligns with the indicators of the 3rd house. To recall, the 3rd house reflects initiation into meditation and spiritual practices. The 5th house supports this by pursuing deep knowledge, wisdom, mantra chanting, etc. The reverse is also true. The 5th house reflects an appreciation for entertainment, and the 3rd house supports this aspect because it reflects music and drama.

With this basic understanding of house systems and bhavas, we can now move on to Siddhant Shastra in the next chapter.

Chapter 5: Siddhant Shastra: Mathematical and Astronomical Principles

We will focus on the basic astronomical and mathematical background of Vedic Astrology. These aspects of Vedic Astrology are described in Siddhant Shastra, which deals primarily with the calculations of lunar and solar months, the speed and distance of planets and constellations, and axes' calculations of the various planets.

The Surya Siddhanta, translated to "The Treatise of the Sun," is a Sanskrit text in Indian Astronomy. With 14 chapters, this 8th-century text describes detailed rules and formulas to calculate the planets' motions relative to the 12 asterisms. It also describes how to calculate the orbits of heavenly bodies.

The Surya Siddhanta asserts that the earth is spherical and that it orbits the sun. It does not mention Uranus and other faraway planets. It is easy to understand this, considering there were no telescopes and viewing these far-off planets was impossible through the naked eye.

Understanding Ayanamsa

Ayan means precession or movement or motion, and Amsha means a "portion" or "part". Ayanamsa translates to a part or portion of the movement (relating to heavenly bodies). Ayanamsa refers to the amount of precession. It stands for the angular difference between the vernal equinox and sidereal Zodiac.

Ayanamsa is the reason there could be differences in calculating Dasas among the various astrologers. Ayanamsa's idea plays an important role in determining divisional charts, determining planetary positions, Dasas, transits, and more. Ayanamsa usage can bring about significant changes in Dasa balances and in high-precision Varga Charts such as Shastiamsa.

We must understand the concept of the preceding equinoxes to improve our understanding of the meaning and effects of Ayanamsa. What are equinoxes? When the celestial equator intersects the ecliptic (or the path of the planets), two points of intersection are created, namely the Spring Equinox and the Fall Equinox.

Spring Equinox falls on March 21st, while the Fall Equinox is on September 21st every year. The Rashis or planets passing through these two equinoxes are continually changing. The Rashis continuously precede these equinoxes, taking 25800 years for all the Rashis to pass through these two equinoxes once. The Rashis get preceded, which is called the *preceding of the equinox.*

Ayanamsa is the difference in the angular distance created each time there is a precession in the equinox. According to Siddhanta Shastra, the precession happens at the rate of one degree every 72 years, which translates to about 50 seconds every year. Ayanamsa can be defined as the difference between tropical (Western) and sidereal (Vedic Astrology) Zodiac. The seemingly small difference is left out for calculations in Western Astrology, whereas it is included in Sidereal or Vedic Astrology leading to more specific calculations, and therefore, increasingly accurate predictions in the latter.

In 285 A.D., the positions of the planets in both the Sidereal and Tropical systems were in sync, which means in that year, there was no Ayanamsa, and there was no precession in that year. In 285 A.D., the planetary positions were the same in both the western and Vedic astrological systems.

But, as precessions started, the differences between the two systems started, and continues to do so, and will continue at the rate of approximately one degree every 72 years. So, in 285 A.D., the ayanamsa was 0, and in 2010, the value was approximately 24 degrees, which means to say, one must subtract the planet position in the tropical version by 24 degrees to arrive at the sidereal length.

The vernal equinox is the position used to measure planetary longitudes and is known as the planet's sayana position. Sayana means "along with the component of differences in degrees". The Nirayana longitude position is obtained after applying the ayanamsa correction to the value of the sayana position. Nirayana means "without the difference in degrees." Western Astrology uses sayana longitudes, whereas followers of Vedic Astrology use the Nirayana system.

An interesting calculation is here to help you understand the impact of Ayanamsa. Approximately 11200 years; hence, the ayanamsa will be exactly the opposite, which means to say, there will be a 180-degree difference between Sidereal and Tropical Astrological System calculations! About 11200 years; if the Sun is positioned in Aries according to the tropical system, the sun will be in Libra, according to Vedic Astrology! Now, that is a big difference, right?

The tropical system superimposes the Zodiac every year on March 21. For western astrology, on March 21st every year, the Sun is always in Aries. The Sidereal system calculates the positions after considering the planets' position behind the Rashi system. These two points differ, resulting in the differences between the predictions made according to your Sun Sign in tropical and Sidereal systems.

The most accepted form of Ayanamsa is the Chitra Paksha ayanamsa proposed by N. C. Lahiri and approved in 1954 by the Astrological Research Institute, Kolkata, India. Most astrologers use this ayanamsa for their calculations. While scholars continue to debate on which is the best and most efficient ayanamsa to follow, as a beginner, you can easily learn about this important element using the Chitra Paksha method.

Here are important terms used in Ayanamsa:

Celestial Latitude - Also called Shar or Vikshep, the celestial latitude is the angular distance of an imaginary arc drawn from the planet to the ecliptic.

Uttarayana - This term refers to the period when Surya enters Makar Rashi and begins his journey towards the north. Uttarayana starts from Makar Sankranti and ends at Mithuna Sankranti. During this period, the duration of daylight time increases with each passing day.

Dakshinayana - This term refers to the period when Surya moves from Karka Sankranti up to Dhanush Sankranti. During the Dakshinayana, the duration of night increases with each passing day.

Equinox - There are two spheres, namely celestial spheres and equators, that intersect each other at 23-degrees, 28-minutes. These two points of intersection are called equinoxes or equinoctial points. One is called the *Vernal Equinox* (Spring Equinox), and the second point of intersection is called *Autumnal* of Fall Equinox.

The Sun revolving in the ecliptic crosses the two celestial spheres twice a year on the equinoxes. On this day, the duration of day and night are equal. The ecliptic changes result in the Sun rising in the northern direction for 6 months (Uttarayana) and in the southern direction for the remaining 6 months (Dakshinayana). As the Sun moves away from the Ayana or from the point of precession, the day's duration increases.

Understanding Dasas

Once you know each of the planets' conditions and strengths, you will know what results you will get from them. But, to know and understand when these results will fructify, you must learn and know about dasas and the transits of the planets through the various Rashis.

So, what are dasas? They are the ruling periods of planets. There are many types of Dasa systems used by astrologers all over. But the most popular, and the most accurate Dasa system is the Vimshottari Dasha System. Let us go into this system in a bit of detail.

You already know that the star constellation in which the moon was passing through becomes your birth Nakshatra. Now, the position and degrees in which this star constellation was placed will determine the dasas that will be in operation right through your lifetime. Here is a chart that details the start of a Dasa, depending on the Nakshatra of your birth. In this chart, we are not considering the movement of the Nakshatra within its 13-degrees, 20-seconds range. The start of the Vimshottari Dasa would have to be adjusted accordingly by reducing the time already passed under the effect of the planet and its lord.

> 1. Ashwini Nakshatra - Ketu Dasa - Vimshottari Dasa period is 7 years
>
> 2. Bharani Nakshatra - Venus (Shukra Dasa) - Vimshottari Dasa period is 20 years
>
> 3. Krittika Nakshatra - Sun (Surya Dasa) - Vimshottari Dasa period is 6 years
>
> 4. Rohini Nakshatra - Moon (Chandra Dasa) - Vimshottari Dasa period is 10 years

5. Mrigashirsha Nakshatra - Mars (Mangala Dasa) - Vimshottari Dasa period is 7 years

6. Ardra Nakshatra - Rahu Dasa - Vimshottari Dasa period is 18 years

7. Punarvasu Nakshatra - Jupiter (Guru Dasa) - Vimshottari Dasa period is 16 years

8. Pushya Nakshatra - Saturn (Shani Dasa) - Vimshottari Dasa period is 19 years

9. Ashlesha Nakshatra - Mercury (Buddha Dasa) - Vimshottari Dasa period is 17 years

10. Magha Nakshatra - Ketu Dasa - Vimshottari Dasa period is 7 years

11. Purva Phalguni - Venus (Shukra Dasa) - Vimshottari Dasa period is 20 years

12. Uttara Phalguni - Sun (Surya Dasa) - Vimshottari Dasa period is 6 years

13. Hasta - Moon (Chandra Dasa) - Vimshottari Dasa period is 10 years

14. Chitra - Mars (Mangala Dasa) - Vimshottari Dasa period is 7 years

15. Swati - Rahu Dasa - Vimshottari Dasa period is 18 years

16. Vishakha - Jupiter (Guru Dasa) - Vimshottari Dasa period is 16 years

17. Anuradha - Saturn (Shani Dasa) - Vimshottari Dasa period is 19 years

18. Jyeshtha - Mercury (Buddha Dasa) - Vimshottari Dasa period is 17 years

19. Moola - Ketu Dasa - Vimshottari Dasa period is 7 years

20. Purvashada - Venus (Shukra Dasa) - Vimshottari Dasa period is 20 years

21. Uttarashada - Sun (Surya Dasa) - Vimshottari Dasa period is 6 years

22. Shravana - Moon (Chandra Dasa) - Vimshottari Dasa period is 10 years

23. Dhanishta - Mars (Mangala Dasa) - Vimshottari Dasa period is 7 years

24. Satabhisha - Rahu Dasa - Vimshottari Dasa period is 18 years

25. Purva Bhadrapada - Jupiter (Guru Dasa) - Vimshottari Dasa period is 16 years

26. Uttara Bhadrapada - Saturn (Shani Dasa) - Vimshottari Dasa period is 19 years

27. Revati - Mercury (Buddha Dasa) - Vimshottari Dasa period is 17 years

The period of each Dasa is given below:

- Surya Dasa is for 6 years
- Chandra Dasa is for 10 years
- Mangala Mars is for 7 years
- Rahu Dasa is for 18 years
- Guru Dasa is for 16 years
- Shani Dasa is for 19 years
- Buddha Dasa is for 17 years
- Ketu Dasa is for 7 years
- Shukra Dasa is for 20 years

Each of the above is called a *mahadasha*. The Vimshottari Dasa follows a period of 120 years of an individual's life. You likely will not experience all the nine mahadashas in your lifetime. Depending on how many degrees the moon has traveled at your birth time, your first mahadasha is reduced proportionately.

Now, every mahadasha is subdivided into dasas of other planets, and these subdivisions are called antardashas. The first antardasha in every mahadasha is that of the mahadasha planet itself, followed by the other planets in their existing sequence. Each antardashas is further subdivided into Pratyantar Dashas, and this process is repeated until we can arrive at the dasas on a daily and even hourly basis. This book does not cover that detail. This is only to indicate to you the deep detailing found in Vedic Astrology.

While the Vimshottari Dasha System is the most prevalent one, you cannot ignore the other dasa systems. Interestingly, although scientifically, there is an agreement in the way stars and planets are placed in our astral system, there are many differences in terms of Ayanamsas and Dasha Systems. A good and well-trained astrologer can synthesize the interpretations of dasas and by including the ayanamsa aspect of Vedic Astrology.

Chapter 6: The First Four: Aries, Taurus, Gemini, and Cancer

From this chapter onwards until Chapter 8, we will be looking at the Zodiac signs in detail. But before that, let us learn about the categories into which the 12 Zodiac signs fall. The 12 Rashis, along with planets and bhavas or houses, form the fundamental elements of Vedic Astrology.

The literal translation of the word "Rashi" is "piling up". Rashis are not divine, and they are not worshipped like the planets are. They are mystical and yet have a deep connection to earthly elements. If you look at the Rashis or Zodiac Signs symbols, they are fish, the balance, scorpion, and other elements that are part of our earthly life. Nakshatras and planets are divine. They are deities, and they are worshipped.

Even if they are not worshipped and are not divine, the Rashis or Zodiac signs hold deep significance in Vedic Astrology. Rashis are compartments in the sky. They are like an environment. As planets move on their ecliptic, they come into these compartments or Rashis, and depending on the Rashi they enter, the planets behave in a certain way.

One of the basic beliefs of Vedic Astrology is called essential dignity, the idea that the nine planets are more effective and powerful in some signs than in others. This is because of the nature of the planet and the Rashi through which it is transiting through are in harmony. But some planets are weak and have difficult effects while passing through some signs because their natures conflict with each other.

Summarily, the effects of planets in each of these Rashis could be favorable or unfavorable to their natural signification. Here is an analogy to help you understand this concept. Suppose you are a spiritual seeker and suddenly find yourself in a pub playing loud, raucous music; you wouldn't like it, right?

Similarly, if a particular planet finds itself in a Rashi that does not conform to its core principle, then unfavorable effects arise. But if a planet finds itself in Rashi or home aligned with its basic nature, then favorable effects arise. The terms used in Vedic Astrology to explain this concept are exaltation (supportive environment and conforming to the planet's objectives and goals resulting in favorable conditions) and debilitation (non-supportive environment for the planet resulting in unfavorable conditions and effects).

Another important aspect of the 12 Zodiac signs is that each has the opposite, resulting in six opposing couples. Fire and Air are opposites just as Earth and Water are opposites. Here are the six opposing couples:

- Aries (Mesha Rashi) is opposite to Libra (Tula Rashi)

- Cancer (Karkata Rashi) is opposite to Capricorn (Makar Rashi)

- Gemini (Mithuna Rashi) is opposite to Sagittarius (Dhanush Rashi)

- Pisces (Meena Rashi) is opposite to Virgo (Kanya Rashi)

• Taurus (Vrishabha Rashi) is opposite to Scorpio (Vrishchika Rashi)

• Leo (Simha Rashi) is opposite to Aquarius (Kumbha Rashi)

Categories by Flexibility

First, the signs are categorized into three types based on their flexibility. The three types include Movable, Fixed, and Dual.

The first type or movable signs (also called *Cardinal signs*) are Aries, Cancer, Libra, and Capricorn, which represent adaptability, movement, activity, quickness, change, reformation, flexibility, letting go and moving on, and dissatisfaction and restlessness.

The second type of fixed signs is Taurus, Leo, Scorpio, and Aquarius. These four signs represent rigidity, gradual but steady, fixed, headstrong nature, resoluteness, determination, dislike towards movement, and rigid opinions.

The third type of the dual signs (also called *mutable signs*) are Gemini, Virgo, Sagittarius, and Pisces. They are of a dual nature and represent a mix of the first and second types. They are oriented towards learning, philosophical, reading, communication, speech, and preaching. They are open to new ideas and are always exploring different opinions. They are good at multitasking.

Categories by Elements

According to the elements, the 12 Zodiac signs are categorized into four types: earth, fire, wind, and water.

The Fire Signs include Aries, Leo, and Sagittarius. They represent energy, assertion, aggression, passion, willpower, leadership, decisiveness, outspokenness, extroversion, hot temperament, active, drive, pioneering, spontaneous, enthusiastic, and impulsive.

The Earth Signs include Taurus, Virgo, and Capricorn. The earth signs represent practicality, caution, methodical and analytical-based approaches, slow and steady, realistic, down-to-earth, accumulating attitude, love reality more than fiction, understand and appreciate the importance and value of materialistic things. They make great planners, organizers, CEOs, directors, etc.

The Air Signs are Gemini, Libra, and Aquarius. They represent intellect, quick-wittedness, abstract thinking, eager learners, communicative, physically active and agile, love to travel and explore, great social skills, philosophical attitude, and a flexible attitude.

The Water Signs are Cancer, Scorpio, and Pisces. They represent emotion, intuition, learning, passion, sensitiveness, hoarding, and collecting both memories and other non-materialistic things and materials and physical things. They are imaginative, introverts, psychic, secretive, and dreamy. They are not very physically agile. They depend on their intuition more than real facts and evidence.

These elements are also given polarity (positive or negative). Air and fire signs are considered positive, and the earth and water signs are considered negative. So, the following can be arrived at with the Zodiac signs' connections with the four elements and polarity.

Categories by Gender

All odd signs are masculine, which means to say, Aries, Gemini, Leo, Libra, Sagittarius, Aquarius are male. Male signs are more pushy, extroverted, communicative, aggressive, destructive attitudes and negative, dominative, and assertive than female Zodiac signs.

All even signs are feminine; Taurus, Cancer, Virgo, Scorpio, Capricorn, Pisces are female. The feminine Zodiac signs are intuitive, quiet, protective, nurturing, emotional, and gentle.

Other Significant Categorizations

Aries, Scorpio, and Capricorn are considered violent signs. Ruled by Saturn and Mars, they tend to be destructive and primarily have a Tamasic nature. When these signs are afflicted in a native's horoscope, these destructive features will be manifested.

Aries, Gemini, Leo, and Virgo are considered barren signs (concerning female fertility). These planets are not fruitful for conception. But Cancer, Scorpio, and Pisces are believed to be fruitful signs.

Shirsodaya Signs are Gemini, Leo, Virgo, Libra, Scorpio, Aquarius, which means planets in these signs manifest their fruits in the first half of their Dasas. Shirsodaya means "rising the head first."

Pristodaya Signs are Aries, Taurus, Cancer, Sagittarius, Capricorn. Translating to "rising with back," the planets' effects in these signs tend to lead to fruition in the second half of their Dasas.

Ubabodaya Signs (means "rising both sides") is Pisces, which means to say that planets in this sign tend to give their effects in the middle half of their dasas.

Let us look at the first four signs of the Zodiac in detail in this chapter.

Aries - Mesha Rashi

Aries is owned by Mars or Mangala. Aries is the Mooltrikona for Mars, who also owns Scorpio. The symbol of Aries is the ram. Aries is an exaltation sign for Mangala (Mars) and a debilitation sign for Saturn or Shani.

Mental Tendencies of People Born in Aries - Aries is a movable, fire, and masculine sign. People born in this sign are active, bold, fearless, pioneering, charismatic, independent, and inspirational. They make great entrepreneurs, leaders, and businessmen being successful at starting new projects, initiatives, and businesses. They love movement and activity. Their frankness and direct approaches can look confident.

But people born in Aries sign be restless and impatient and find it difficult to sustain energy and interest in their ventures for long periods. They can get aggressive and dominating. Their confidence and frankness could come across as domineering and unpleasant. They are selfish and tend to look only for their own interests more often than not.

Physical Appearance - Individuals born in Mesha Rashi usually have a lean, muscular physique. They have a ruddy complexion with a long neck and face. Their faces are usually broad at the temples and narrow towards the chin. With bushy eyebrows and wiry or rough hair, Aries people often go bald.

Health - Amply supported with the power to resist diseases, Arians typically enjoy good health. They are prone to head injuries that could range from minor to very serious. Them should avoid rash driving. Arians are also likely to suffer from burns, headaches, brain afflictions, inflammatory diseases, pimples, insomnia, and paralysis.

Basic Cautionary Advice - Arians should make sure they get plenty of rest and sleep. They should learn to relax and keep their feelings in exchange, especially anger, worry, and excitement. Stimulants and meat should be avoided while healthy, organic food and vegetables should be included in their daily diets.

Taurus - Vrishabha Rashi

The planet lord of the Taurus sign is Venus. Taurus is a fixed, earth, and feminine sign. The symbol of Taurus is the bull. Taurus is a sign of exaltation for Chandra or the Moon. It is not a debilitation sign for any planet.

Mental Tendencies of People Born Under Taurus Sign - People born in the Taurus Sign are loyal, sensual, down to earth, practical, and stable individuals. They are the kind who believe in slow and steady winning the race. Their determination and perseverance hold them in good stead right through their lives.

They are passionate about and love material possessions. Being conservative, Taureans are highly dedicated and faithful to their home, family, and relationships. They are stubbornly loyal towards their loved ones. Most of the time, they demonstrate a calm and peaceful personality. But they often get agitated when pestered beyond their limits. Taureans can be secretive, violent, unrelenting, and unreasonably stubborn and adamant.

Physical Appearance - Taureans are typically short to average height. They have a broad forehead and are plump with a stout, thick neck. They have a clear complexion, dark hair, and a very well-developed body.

Health - People born under this Rashi usually are blessed with great health and are less sensitive to physical pain than many other people. They rarely admit to physical pains and disability, and if they fall ill, then they have a long and painful recovery period because their recuperative powers are quite low. Taureans are prone to afflictions of the throat and neck.

Basic Cautionary Advice - They should learn not to be overly obstinate. They should work on the slowness of their actions. Being unselfish, non-vindictive, and letting go of anger will also help Taureans lead a happier life than otherwise.

Gemini - Mithuna Rashi

The planet lord owning Gemini or Mithuna Rashi is Mercury or Buddha. Gemini is a dual, air, and masculine sign. The symbol of Gemini is a pair of twins. Mithuna Rashi is a sign of exaltation for Rahu and a sign of debilitation for Ketu.

Mental Tendencies of Gemini-Borns - People born in this sign are communicative, highly intellectual, and do everything, including think, talk, and walk fast. They usually have a pedantic nature and love learning. With excellent writing and reading skills, people of the Gemini sign are clever and versatile. They can multitask well and are adaptable and flexible.

They are witty and bring humor to a group. They love change and diversity, even in their routine life. They can be good in information and data-related fields. But they have different personalities under varied conditions. While their oratory skills are great, they may take on an argumentative approach.

Basic Cautionary Advice - Plenty of rest and sleep is important for Geminis. They should also exercise well, make sure they get fresh air regularly, eat conservatively, and work on building mental peace.

Cancer - Karka Rashi

Chandra or the Moon owns cancer or Karkata Rashi. Cancer is a movable, water, and female sign. Cancer's symbol is the crab and is a sign of exaltation for Guru or Jupiter and a sign of debilitation for Mangala or Mars.

Mental tendencies of Cancerians - People born in the sign of Cancer are emotional, motherly, intuitive, nurturing, and protective. They have excellent memory skills and can save and recall memories of people and objects. With a sympathetic and caring attitude, Cancerians are loved by those around them. Although they love traveling, they do so only if they know they can return to a stable, happy home.

They love domesticated home life and find security in a family environment. They are devoted to their families. They are most hospitable and timid. But they can get aggressive if loved ones are threatened. They have good business instincts, and their ability to learn and imbibe new knowledge is strong. They are honest but are highly impressionable.

Health - They have fragile health during their youth but usually become healthier as they age. They are prone to chest and stomach problems. They must take care of their weakness of being excessively nervous and worried.

Basic Cautionary Advice - They should learn to be patient. Their changing and indolent attitude must be corrected. They should avoid inferiority complexes and become more practical in their life. They should work towards overcoming passiveness, anxiety, and laziness.

Chapter 7: The Middle Earth: Leo, Virgo, Libra, and Scorpio

This chapter deals with the middle four Zodiac signs, namely Leo, Virgo, Libra, and Scorpio. Read on to discover more about each.

Leo - Simha Rashi

The owner of Leo or Simha Rashi is Sun or Surya. Leo is a fixed, fire, and masculine sign. The symbol of Leo is the lion. Simha Rashi is not a sign of exaltation or debilitation for any planet.

Mental tendencies of Leos - People born in this sign have great leadership abilities, are royal, noble, and proud. The Leonines want attention, and they get it; they are as tame as a domestic cat when loved, but can turn into a lion when ignored.

They are outspoken, honest, extroverted, frank, and intense. Leos are confident, independent, and dynamic. They are intelligent and brilliant with great innovative skills. They may be stubborn and ambitious beyond reasonable measure. They love being complimented. They are helpful and have a protective and fatherly attitude towards their friends and loved ones.

Although they are fearless and energetic, they can become pushy in an unpleasantly aggressive way. They are always dogmatic in their approach with others and become annoyingly dominating. Their argumentative nature gets them into trouble with people, especially their superiors and bosses.

Physical Appearance - With broad shoulders, large-sized bones, and muscles, the body of a Leo-born individual usually has a better-formed upper-part than the lower part. Leos have a thin waist and prominent knees. They have soft and wavy hair, although they go bald. A majestic and imposing appearance commands dignity and respect.

Health - Leos have splendid health and rarely fall ill. Even if they do, they recover rapidly from their sickness. But they get alarmed when they become sick or ill, and if the illness is not responding to treatment quickly enough for Leos. The diseases indicated for Leos are heart-related and nerve-related.

Basic Precautionary Advice - Leos should avoid enforcing their opinions and ideas on others and be careful of getting excessively dominating. They should work at taking others' views and suggestions before deciding on any issue. They should hold back their temperamental and hasty nature and remember not to be carried away by flattery.

Virgo - Kanya Rashi

Virgo is the Mooltrikona sign and is owned by Mercury or Buddha, who also owns Gemini. Rahu is also a co-ruler of Virgo. Virgo's symbol is the maiden. Virgo is a dual female sign connected to the earth element. Kanya Rashi is a sign of exaltation for its own lord, namely Mercury, and a sign of debilitation for Shukra or Venus.

Mental Tendencies of Virgo - People born in the Virgo sign are analytical and have a quantitative approach to everything. They are intelligent, deep thinkers, and research-oriented. They are also practical and down to earth. They admire a clean, hygienic, and orderly environment. They are perfectionists and can be quite critical of relentless problems and problematic people. Virgo-born individuals are highly methodical and are ingenious. They are quite precise in their work, although they get nervous and undecided about many things.

They have excellent trade and business instincts. They are good mathematics and are exceedingly orderly and systematic. People born in the Virgo are very hardworking and are continuously striving to do their best. Virgoans lack self-confidence.

Physical Appearance - With dark, curly hair, people born under the Virgo sign usually have a slender body. They have a thin, shrill voice. They walk fast and rarely get a pot-belly. They have a straight nose and, most often, look younger than their real age. They have a pronounced forehead and use honest, frank expressions. Their complexion depends on the ascendant planet and aspects of that planet.

Health - People born under the Virgo sign usually enjoy robust health and live to a ripe, old age. They are active and appear younger than they are, especially in their youth. They are quite particular about their health, too. Virgo-born individuals are prone to stomach and nerve problems.

Basic Precautionary Advice - They should learn to be less talkative and less impulsive, first think before deciding, and be less fickle-minded. They should also learn to forget and forgive others' mistakes. Virgos must avoid discontentment, worries, short temper, and irritability.

Libra - Tula Rashi

Libra is the Mooltrikona sign and is owned by Venus or Shukra, who also owns Taurus. Libra's symbol is the balancing scales. Libra is a male, movable sign related to the air element. Librans are pleasant and balanced. Tula Rashi is a sign of exaltation for Shani or Saturn and a sign of debilitation for Surya or Sun.

Mental Tendencies of Librans - They are very cooperative in a group - as well as social and friendly. Librans are perfectionists and have a deep sense of justice and harmony. They are highly creative, born in the Libra sign, lovers of the arts, including music and literature. They admire the beauty and enjoy social settings. They are courteous and hospitable too.

They are quite charming, diplomatic, and ever-smiling, making them popular and highly likable among many people and friends. They make good judgments of both people and situations quickly. They can be extravagant as they love to live in the lap of luxury. They are excellent at crowd management, have great organizing skills, and might be pushy, though in a pleasant way. Their short-temper may be a big problem for them.

Physical Appearance - With a well-formed body, good complexion, Libras put on weight during their middle age. They have smooth, desirable features, although their body contours and curves can be irregular. They are good-looking, graceful people with an attractive countenance. They look younger than their actual age.

Health - Librans are usually healthy, though they may be prone to infectious diseases. Their Achilles heel in terms of health include kidneys, loins, pineal glands, spinal cord, etc. They should take care of these parts. Diseases indicated for Librans include polyuria, appendicitis, and lumbago.

Basic Cautionary Advice - Librans must learn to control their emotions, especially when they are in a giving mood. They let things go out of hand during such times and give away more than they should. They should learn to say NO to people. Their liberal behavior makes them easy targets for others to take advantage of them.

Scorpio - Vrishchika Rashi

Scorpio or Vrishchika Rashi has two rulers, including Mars or Mangala and Ketu. Scorpio is a fixed, masculine Zodiac sign related to the water element. Scorpio's symbol is the scorpion, the reason why this Rashi is sometimes referred to as "Keeta". Scorpio is not a sign of exaltation for any planet while it is a sign of debilitation for Chandra or Moon.

Mental Tendencies of Scorpions - People born in the Scorpio sign are secretive, passionate, focused, intense, and determined individuals. But they can be obsessive and unyielding, with particularly strong likes & dislikes. Scorpions find it difficult to remain idle, and they work best when faced with hurdles and obstacles. They never surrender and fight to the end.

They may be outwardly calm even when undergoing inner turmoil, thanks to their strong emotions and complex imaginative skills. They are moody and temperamental and do not forget and forgive easily. They can be good friends but also be the worst enemy. Therefore, they never have lifelong friends.

They are quite cunning and excellent detectives, considering their ability to hide their true emotions and personality. They also have good psychic skills. However, they get quite jealous and cling on to revengeful feelings. Although they are stubborn, people born in Scorpio are charismatic and self-made individuals.

Interestingly, the Scorpio sign represents two types - the higher type with great control over their senses and the lower type of Scorpios who are rude, jealous, and irreconcilable seekers of materialistic pleasure.

Physical Appearance - With a well-proportioned body, Scorpions generally are good-looking. They are average stature, broad, and a commanding presence. They usually gravitate towards being stout and are typically square-faced. Most are of dusky complexion unless their ascendant is affected by a malefic planet(s).

Health - Diseases and problems for Scorpions are found in the bladder, pelvic bone, prostate glands, seminal vesicles, and others. They could be affected by brain afflictions, coma, neuralgia, insomnia, and somnambulism.

Basic Precautionary Advice - Scorpions need to control their sarcasm and overly critical attitude. They should avoid selfishness and secret animosity. The negative aspect of Scorpio is its ability to create anarchy and destruction. It is best to know this failing and work towards avoiding your personality to take on these habits.

Chapter 8: The Heaven Above: Sagittarius, Capricorn, Aquarius, and Pisces

This chapter deals with the final four signs of the Zodiac. Read on to discover more about these four.

Sagittarius - Dhanush Rashi

Sagittarius or Dhanush Rashi is owned by Jupiter or Guru, who also owns Pisces. Sagittarius' Mooltrikona is Sagittarius. The symbol of Sagittarius is the archer, and sometimes, the Centaur represents it. Dhanush Rashi is a sign of exaltation for Ketu and a sign of debilitation for Rahu.

Mental Tendencies of Sagittarius - Sagittarius is a dual, masculine sign connected to the fire element. People born in the Sagittarius sign are outspoken, bold, and optimistic individuals. They can look at the positive side of all things, regardless of how tough or difficult a situation might be. They are best when faced with hurdles and obstacles. They are blessed with an abundance of vigor, vitality, energy, and enthusiasm.

They are idealistic in their outlook and love traveling. They are attracted to spirituality and religion and have strong faith. They are determined and even pushy to an extent. But they are very jovial, just, and friendly people. They can put on a business-like behavior, although they end up promising more than they can deliver.

Their communication style is expansive and outspoken. They can be blunt to a fault. They love to preach and teach and do well in the fields of law. medicine, teaching, and religion.

Physical Appearance - With a well-developed and well-proportioned physique, people born under the Sagittarius sign are tall and slender with either a long or an oval face. They have a large forehead and bushy or high eyebrows. They have expressive eyes and a charming presence. They bald early, especially near the temples.

Health - The body parts about health and diseases are thighs, hips, buttocks, etc. Therefore, diseases indicated are hip fractures, rheumatism, gout, lung troubles, etc.

Basic Precautionary Advice - Sagittarians should be careful not to hurt or insult others with their overly frank and outspoken way of communicating. It is not important that they do not develop enmity towards their parents and siblings. They are likely to fail at the home front and not get the independence they seek in their domestic life. So, adjustment would be required. It is also necessary not to exaggerate and talk non-stop using lies, undeliverable promises, and to insult or hurt others.

Capricorn - Makar Rashi

Saturn or Shani owns Capricorn or Makar Rashi. Capricorn is a movable female sign connected to the earth element. Capricorn's symbol is the goat. Capricorn is a sign of exaltation for Mangala or Mars and a sign of debilitation for Guru or Jupiter.

Mental Tendencies of Capricorn-Born Individuals - People born in Capricorn are practical, prudent, intelligent, and down-to-earth individuals. They are serious, orthodox, and reserved people. They are very methodical and persistently plod through their tasks.

They love to travel. With their high levels of perseverance, they rise to the top slowly but steadily and become self-made individuals. They have keen business skills, organizational skills, and managerial ability. Capricorn people are thoughtful, patient, and tolerant of others. They do not trust those around them easily. They are capricious and desirous of power, authority, and wealth.

Physical Appearance - With a prominent, long, and thin nose, people born in the sign of Capricorn are commonly short at their young age but become tall suddenly after 16 years. They are likely to become hunch-backed with advancing age. They usually have a defect while walking.

Basic Precautionary Advice - They must learn not to be very pessimistic, egoistic, and selfish. They should learn not to become broken-hearted or desperate. Avoid overworking and take rest to maintain physical and mental health. The people born in this sign should be careful not to get carried away by discontentment and undue nervousness.

Aquarius - Kumbh Rashi

Aquarius or Kumbh Rashi is owned by Shani, for whom this is the Mooltrikona too. Also, Rahu is the co-ruler of Aquarius. The symbol of Aquarius is the water-bearer. Aquarius is a fixed, masculine Zodiac sign representing the air element. Kumbh Rashi is not a sign of exaltation or debilitation for any planet.

Mental Tendencies of Kumbh Rashi Individuals - People born in the Aquarius sign are abstract thinkers. They are socially conscious individuals. Like the people born in Capricorn, those born in Aquarius are also serious and thoughtful but are more communicative. They are stubborn and are rigid in thinking. They do not like moving and changing situations. They have a scientific and research-oriented bent of mind. They are hard workers with excellent organization skills.

They are extraordinarily intelligent and inventive and can think ahead of time. They are creative and make friends easily, but have strong likes and dislikes. They are highly altruistic and unselfish. They are also rebellious and love to preach about change, although they themselves are resistant to changes of any kind. They have great self-control too. They have strong, innovative ideas and are self-thinking individuals. They can be stubborn, but they are not foolhardy.

Physical Appearance - People born in this sign generally have a tall stature. They have a well-developed, strong physique and become a bit stout during their middle years. But they have a handsome, pleasing personality.

Health - Kumbh Rashi people are highly susceptible to infectious diseases. They could also have heart-related afflictions, including rheumatism and blood pressure.

Basic Precautionary Advice - If any other planet's adverse aspect afflicts the ascendant planet or Saturn, then the native is likely to be lazy and lethargic. Such people should cultivate hard work and be active and prompt. They should not be alone and worry excessively. Avoid pessimism and gloominess. They should also take care of being unreasonably rigid about their likes and dislikes.

Pisces - Meena Rashi

Jupiter owns Pisces or Meena Rashi. Pisces is a dual, feminine sign connected to the water element. Pisces' symbol is the fish. The Pisces sign is a sign of exaltation for Venus or Shukra and a sign of debilitation for Mercury or Buddha.

Mental Tendencies of Pisces-Born Individuals - People born in the Pisces sign are emotional, sensitive, and quite impressionable. Pisceans tend to be dreamy and romantic with a kind, charitable, and a giving and forgiving attitude. They are fond of music and arts and are somewhat disconnected from reality. They are weak in physical and mental activity and trust others easily. They are philosophical and have a passionate attitude towards life.

They can be moody and temperamental and yet have a spiritual and meditative approach to life and its problems. They like being alone and often get into a reflective mood. They are forgetful and have a tendency to have dreams and psychic visions. They are friendly and softly magnetic and have a happy-go-lucky attitude. They have a liberal outlook, but lack confidence and determination. They may get indecisive to that extent.

Physical Appearance - Pisceans usually have a plump body and a short stature. They have a fleshy face and a tendency for a double chin. Their shoulders are spherical and muscular.

Health - Pisceans could be addicted to drinking. Health indicators for them include gastric troubles and varicose veins. Liver and feet afflictions are also indicated.

Basic Precautionary Advice - Pisceans are easily impressed, and therefore, they could end up befriending people putting up pretenses, thus harming themselves. So, it is important for individuals born in the sign of Pisces to take care and be choosy while making friends. Pisceans also need to learn to be pushy. They can be generous but should be warned about being overly liberal.

Chapter 9: Divisional Charts

Now that you have the basics of planets, stars, and Rashis in place, we can move on to predictive astrology using a unique technique of Vedic Astrology called *Divisional Charts*. The credit of the success to make accurate predictions is largely contributed by these Divisional Charts, which are also known as *Varga Charts*.

Varga is a Sanskrit term meaning "division" called a *Zodiac sign or Rashi division*. Each division or fractional part is called an "*amsa*". Here is a simple explanation for you. You already know that each Zodiac sign has 30-degrees in its space. In these charts, this sign of 30-degrees is further subdivided into different numbers of equal divisions or amsas.

Each planet is again mapped in each of these amsas resulting in Divisional Charts of a native. Each amsa has an influence on the native's life. Vedic Astrology uses 16 Vargas or divisional charts resulting in a unique system to find the auspicious and inauspicious effects of planets.

The Parashara System of Astrology uses these 16 divisional charts for predictive astrology. In the Rashi chart, the 12 regions correspond to the 12 Zodiac signs. If there are two divisions, then it means each house or regions is divided into two amsas or parts, resulting in 24 regions. And this goes on.

- **The Rashi Chart** (only one division) called *D1* is used to predict details about the native's physical matters, including his body, status of health, and other general matters. The Rashi Chart is the basic one where the study of a native's horoscope begins.

- **The Hora Chart** (with 2 divisions) called *D2* deals with wealth and family. The D2 helps to understand the financial position and matters of the native. A strong position of the Sun in this chart means the quantity of wealth owned by the native will be very good. If the Moon has a strong position, earning money will be easy for the native.

- **The Drekkana Chart** (with three divisions) dealing with siblings and the nature of the native is called *D3*. Planets in certain divisions of this chart can bode badly. For example, if planets are in the Sarpa Drekkana, then it is not considered good for the native's health condition.

- **The Chaturthamsa Chart** (with four divisions) called *D4* deals with matters relating to fortune and property.

- **The Saptamsa Chart** (with seven divisions) called *D7* deals with the aspects of children and progeny.

- **The Navamsa Chart** (with nine divisions) called *D9* is used to predict the spouse (or wife), dharma, and the relationships of the concerned native. After the Rashi Chart, the Navamsa Chart is the most important one used in predictive Vedic Astrology. If a planet is exalted in the Rashi Chart but debilitated in D9, then the planet may not be beneficial. Interestingly, the lord of the 64th division in D9 is an indicator of longevity and Marala Dasa (connected to death) of the native.

- **The Dasamsa Chart** (with ten divisions) called *D10* deals with the native's profession and his or her interactions in society.

- **Dvadamsa Chart** (with 12 divisions) or *D12* deals with parents

- **Shodasamsa Chart** (with 16 divisions) or *D16* is for traveling, vehicles, and comforts.

- **Vimsamsa Chart** (with 20 divisions) or *D20* is for spiritual pursuits.

- **Chatur Vimsamsa Chart** (with 24 divisions) or *D24* is for education, knowledge, and learning.

- **Sapta Vimsamsa Chart** (with 27 divisions) or *D27* is for the strengths and weaknesses of the native.

- **Trimsamsa Chart** (with 30 divisions) or *D30* is for evils, bad luck, and failures.

- **Khavedamsha Chart** (with 40 divisions) or *D40* 0s for maternal legacy.

- **Akshavedamsa Chart** (with 45 divisions) or *D45* is for paternal legacy.

- **Shastiamsa Chart** (with 60 divisions) or *D60* is for part births and karma

Besides the above 16 Vargas attributed to Parashara, there are four more attributed to Jaimini. These four Vargas or divisional charts include:

1. **Panchamsa** (with five divisions) is called *D5* and represents fame and power.

2. **Shasthamsa** (with six divisions) is called *D6,* which represents health.

3. **Ashtamsa** (with eight divisions), or *D8* representing unexpected troubles.

4. **Ekadasamsa or Rudramsa** (with 11 divisions) representing death and destruction.

The biggest challenge in drawing up such detailed divisional charts is that the exact time of a person's birth is rarely obtained. Even a minute difference in noting the time of birth could affect the accuracy. The accurate time of birth is essential because otherwise, the Lagna and other planetary positions can change significantly, resulting in wrong the charts being used to make predictions. But there are cases, especially when the father is a doctor and attended the birth, when correct times of birth have been recorded. Then it is possible to create precise charts for the native.

Of all the above charts, the Rashi Chart is the primary, and all the other divisional charts and information received from them relate to this. For example, if Jupiter is in the Mool Trikona in the Rashi chart and it is in a sign of debilitation in D10 or the Dasamsa chart, which deals with the native's profession and career. The debilitated Jupiter should give you an indication that the native could be a bad boss whom people fear and hate at his or her workplace. The 10th house and the lord of the 10th house in the D10 chart is important for career-related predictions.

In all the divisional charts, the Kendra houses are the most important ones. If the Kendra houses have good planets in them, then the native's career is likely to do well. So, analyzing the Rashi chart will give you inputs about the native's profession or career, while the analysis of the D10 will give you insights into the progress and quality.

Continuing further, the benefic planets are depending on the Lagna. So, for a correct and full analysis of a native's career, you would need to check the Lagna, the Sun and Moon positions, and the 10th house from the Lagna. The same procedure should be used for accurate predictions of other aspects of a native's life using the other divisional charts.

Planets become increasingly benefic and auspicious if they occupy the same Zodiac house in the 16 divisional charts. The planets get graded based on this element. If a planet is stationed in its own sign or the Mooltrikona sign or in any other good sign in two of the 16 Vargas, it is said to have achieved Parijat Amsa.

If the planet acquires this condition in any three divisional charts, it is said to have achieved Uttam Amsa. This gradation of a planet increases with the number of Vargas with this condition, and the status names for each planet are:

- In four Vargas - Gopuramsa
- In five Vargas - Simhasana amsa
- In six Vargas - Paravatmasa
- In seven Vargas - Devlok amsa
- In eight Vargas - Kumkumamsa
- In nine Vargas - Iravatamsa
- In ten Vargas - Vaishnavamsa
- In 11 Vargas - Saivamsa
- In 12 Vargas - Bhaswadansa
- In 13 Vargas - Vaisheshikamsa
- In 14 Vargas - Indrasanamsa
- In 15 Vargas - Golokamsa
- In 16 Vargas - Shrivallabhamsa

Implication and Importance of Divisional Charts

Divisional charts are essential for a detailed analysis of any horoscope. One of the primary purposes is to note the placement of a planet in different charts. If a particular planet is in a strong position in many divisions, then it is strong. If it is in weak places, then the planet is rendered weak.

A planet located in one Zodiac sign or Rashi by itself is called a *"yoga"* or an *"avayoga"* because of the relationship the planet establishes with the lord of that Rashi as well as the lords of the other related Rashis, especially in connection with Lagna. It is important to note that the mere occupation of a planet in a Rashi will not produce the results or effects in accordance with that occupation.

This is because no planet can act alone. Every planet establishes active relationships with one or more other planets and the Rashi it occupies, and Varga-wise status gained by the planet and multiple other factors. If a yoga fails to give the expected result, then the reason could be anything. For example, it could be the Varga-wise weakness of the planet rather than the planet itself.

Let us take an example to understand this concept. The Sun in the 9th house not in any hostile sign gives wealth, friends, piety, and children to the native, although this position can drive antagonism towards the father and wife, having reduced happiness. If the Sun is the Lagna lord and is in the exalted 9th house, then the native and his father could have a great relationship, and there need not be any reduction in happy times. So, the expected negative results are counted by other factors as defined from the divisional charts.

Following are more examples of using Divisional Charts for predictions.

Planets in Navamsa Affecting Future Life - The Navamsa chart or D9 represents spouse and marriage and the dignity of planets. This chart must be consulted for matters related to marriage, besides its being one of the most important divisional charts used for other predictions. D9 is important because it is seen as the fruit if D1 or the Rashi chart is the tree. The Navamsa signifies the authentic dignity of a planet because it stands for the planets giving their effects or fruits through its Dasas.

From a philosophical context, D9 represents the thought process the native would develop after he or she experiences life and learns from these events. There arises the concept of D9 triggering future life, or at least later in the current dasa. And the same logic supports the idea that a planet in a strong position in D9 is bound to give better results later in time or later during its dasa. The Navamsa will depict your learning from the life lessons the planet offered you.

Another key element to remember is that the idea of exaltation and debilitation signs are more significant in D1 than in any other divisional chart. According to Sage Parashara, the exaltation or debilitation signs and specific degrees are clearly defined. For example, Chandra is exalted in the 2nd pada of Krittika, which is the first Navamsa of Taurus. In the 2nd Navamsa of Taurus becomes the Mooltrikona of Chandra.

In Navamsa or any other divisional chart, the second pada of Krittika does not fall after the first pada of Krittika. So, with exaltation and debilitation, the lengths or degrees become immaterial. Only the D1 should be considered for this aspect. Therefore, in this particular case, Chandra in the second pada of Krittika will not result in anything bad in later life or in the later part of Chandra Dasa.

Another point of interest is that if a planet is weak in the Rashi Chart, its position is not improved significantly, even if it is in a solid position in any of the divisional charts. The reverse is, but different. If a planet is in a strong position, its strength is reduced if it is placed in a position of debilitation in the Divisional Chart under consideration.

Here is an example to illustrate this. Suppose your Rashi Chart has the lord of the 10th house in an exalted position. If the concerned astrologer has predicted good fortune in your career based on this without checking the relevant divisional chart, then this prediction may not come true. Maybe the same planet is in a debilitation sign in the D10 (divisional career chart). So, correct predictions, in this case, can be obtained only by checking and verifying both the D1 and D10 charts.

In summary, we can say this about Divisional Charts. The Rashi Charts are like the human body, which gives you a general understanding of a person's life. If you want detailed ways of how the internal systems are working, you would have to do ECG or biopsy or other tests concerned with that particular part, right? The Divisional Charts are like these detailed studies that give you information about specific areas of your life.

Chapter 10: Planetary Strengths and Avasthas

After Divisional Charts, we will focus on another powerful predictive technique used in Vedic Astrology, namely Planetary Strengths. The various longitudinal-based positioning of the planets combined with a concept called "*six-fold strength*" is a powerful tool used for higher prediction levels.

Let us start by understanding what *avastha* is. It is an important concept in the world of Vedic Astrology. Avastha in Sanskrit translates to "stage," "state," or "level." It refers to the state or stage of planets. There are many types of avasthas, the most basic one highly useful for beginners being the "Baladi Avastha".

In the odd Zodiac signs, namely Aries, Gemini, Leo, Libra, Sagittarius, and Aquarius, any planet is in the following avasthas according to the degrees:

> • 0-6 degrees - The planet is said to be in its infancy avastha, during which time it will have minimal effects on the native.

- 6-12 degrees - The planet is said to be in adolescence avastha, and during this period, its entire potential effects can be experienced.

- 12-18 degrees - In this mature state, the planet will render its full potential.

- 18-24 degrees - In this old stage, the planet will have limited effects.

- 24-30 degrees - During the last 6-degrees of a Zodiac (near-death state), the planet will have very minimal effects, if any.

In the even Zodiac signs, namely Taurus, Cancer, Virgo, Scorpio, Capricorn, and Pisces, the planets are in the following avasthas as per the longitudinal degrees:

- 0-6 degrees - Near-death avastha

- 6-12 degrees - Old avastha

- 12-18 degrees - mature avastha

- 18-24 degrees - adolescent avastha

- 24-30 degrees - near-death avastha

These degree measurements mustn't be taken literally but considered liberally. According to degrees, this differentiation implies that planets somewhat in the center of a Zodiac sign (between 12 - 18 degrees) render their maximum effects. A planet towards the ends of the signs tend to blend into the next or previous sign and is not very deeply colored by the current Rashi. From a mathematical perspective, the 15-degrees point is at the dead center of a sign, and is most affected by the characteristics of that sign.

Significance of Residential Strength of a Planet

Every horoscope has a rising sign called the Lagna or the ascendant. It is one of the 12 Zodiac signs, of course. But, according to the precise time of birth, the Lagna will have an exact degree within that sign between 0 and 30. This degree becomes an important point of every sign for that native's horoscope.

Let us take an example. Suppose the ascendant sign is Capricorn at 20-degrees for a person. This 2nd house for this person would be Aquarius. The 20th degree of the second house will be the exact center of the 2nd bhaav, which represents speech, family, wealth, money, etc.

A planet in any sign at exactly 20-degrees of a house will have 100% of residential strength and give its full potential of effects. The strength of the bhaav will be good between 15 and 25 degrees (plus or minus 5 degrees). Beyond this limit, the bhaav of that sign will decrease with every degree away from 20-degrees.

In the same example, if a planet is at 4-degrees of a particular sign, according to the Baladi Avastha, it belongs to the previous sign. For example, if a planet is at 2 degrees in Aquarius (the 2nd sign), then although it is in the 2nd house, the bhaav of the previous sign will be in effect.

Significance of Nakshatra Placement

To reiterate, there are 12 Zodiac signs of 30-degrees each and 27 Nakshatras or asterisms of 13-degrees, 20-minutes each. These 27 Nakshatras are ruled by the nine planets, namely Ketu, Shukra, Surya, Chandra, Mangala, Rasu, Guru, Shani, and Buddha (the first nine asterisms respectively). The same sequence of planet lords is then maintained for the next 9 Nakshatras, and again for the third set of nine Nakshatras.

The above situation means every one of the nine planets rules over three Nakshatras equidistant from each other. You already know that the Nakshatra in which the Moon is housed at the time of a person's birth becomes the birth Nakshatra of the native. Planets in the 3rd, 5th, and 7th Nakshatras from the birth Nakshatra of a person will be weak and give malefic effects to him or her. Planets in the 2nd, 6th, and 9th asterisms will give beneficial effects, and the planets in the 1st, 4th, and 8th asterisms will be neutral, although slightly skewed towards giving positive effects for the native in question.

Significance of Planetary Strengths in Varga Charts

Sage Parashara, in addition to defining the 16 Varga Charts, also gave a weighted scheme to attribute the importance of these charts to analyze horoscopes and make predictions. This weighted scheme is useful to obtain a quantitative analysis of the effects of the planets using scores for each planet obtained through this scheme. Higher the score of a planet, the better the results of that particular in its Vimshottari Dasa. High scores reflect the fructification powers of the planet under consideration.

The weighted scheme given by Sage Parashara uses only six of the 16 divisional charts and is:

       1. Rashi Chart (D1) - 6 points

       2. Hora Chart (D2) - 2 points

       3. Drekkana Chart (D3) - 4 points

       4. Navamsa Chart (D9) - 5 points

       5. Dwadasamsa Chart (D12) - 2 points

       6. Trimsamsa Chart (D30) - 1 point

Every planet has a total potential score of 20 points. To reiterate, the exaltation and debilitation effects of planets in divisional charts do not hold value. The following sequence of houses denotes the decreasing value of beneficial effects offered by any planet:

1. Mooltrikona house

2. Own house

3. Best friend house

4. Friend house

5. Neutral house

6. Enemy house

7. Great enemy house

Sage Parashara also defined the weightage for each of the above placements of planets. Let us use an example to illustrate this weightage scheme used in Vedic Astrology. Suppose Mooltrikona is 100%, 90% to own house, and so forth. Next, suppose a planet is housed in the Mooltrikona in D1 and its own house in D9, in the house of a best friend in another divisional chart, and so forth. Then, the weightage scheme looks like this: 100% of 6 + 90% of 5 +.......... (similar contributions from the other six divisional charts to be filled here) to take the total score out of 20.

This total from the weightage scheme will give you a numeric value, which is a good indicator of how the planet will behave in its Vimshottari Dasa. The reason for Sage Parashara to use this weightage scheme is quite evident. As you already know, the Varga charts represent the different aspects of our life. For example, D1 gives a general outlook on a native's life, D9 is for marriage and spouse, D3 is for siblings, D10 is for career, etc. all of which are the support systems of our life. So, the planet's position reflects the depth and level of these support systems. The better the numerical score, the better the beneficial effects of that planet.

Shadbala - The Six-Fold Strength in Vedic Astrology

Any planet or *Graha* gets strength from various sources, including the Rashi, Varga, Bhava, Day or nighttime, Krishna/Shukla Paksha, and more. Krishna Paksha is the fortnight that starts from the full moon day (Poornima) to the new moon day (Amavasya). Shukla Paksha is the other fortnight that starts from the new moon day until the full moon day.

Shadbala is a mathematical system used to quantify the strength of a planet attained through six sources. This number representing the strength of a planet is an important tool to understand the real impact of the concerned planet on the different aspects of a native's life. Detailed and extensive explanations of assessing a planet's strength are given in the Brihat Parashara Hora Shastras. The unit of strength is measured in Virupas.

The mathematical computation given by Sage Parashara is quite complex and layered. But most experienced astrologers can quickly assess the strength of a planet by making a mental model. Let us look at the six sources of strength used in Shadbala.

- **Sthana Bala** - The strength of a planet drawn from the various positions and stations it takes in the Rashi Chart and other Varga charts are called *Sthana Bala* or strength from the occupied place.

- **Dik Bala** - This source of strength of a planet is drawn from its placements in specific Kendras.

- **Kala Bala** - The strength of a planet that depends on the time of an event or the birth of a person is called Kalabala.

- **Chesta Bala** - The strength drawn from the movement of the planet is called *Chestbala*. The movement of a planet means whether it is moving fast, slow, forward, or reverse.

• **Naisargika Bala** - This source of strength is depending on the natural power (or strengths) and weakness of a planet.

• **Drgbala** - The strength drawn from the malefic and benefic planet is called *drgbala*. The benefic planets (or shubh grahas) are sources of strength, whereas a malefic planet (or papa Graha) is a source of weakness.

Let us look at each strength in detail.

Sthana Bala or the Positional Strength of a Planet

The Sthana Bala of a planet is based on its "placement" or "position" as explained above and represents the "place" factor. "Sthana" in Sanskrit translates to "place". The maximum Sthana Bala strength a planet can achieve is 390 Virupas comprising of the strengths derived from the six components discussed below:

1. **Uccha Bala** - This position indicates the distance of the planet from its deepest exaltation point. The closer is this distance, the stronger the effects of the planet. Maximum strength - 30 virupas

2. **Saptavargaja Bala** - This indicates the power of a planet in seven divisional charts, including the Rashi Hora Drekkana Saptamsa, Navamsa, Dwadasamsa, and Trimvimsa. Maximum strength - 225 Virupas

3. **Ojayuggama Bala** - Oja translates to male or odd, and yumna means female or even. This type of Sthana bala is sourced from male and female planets placed in male and female Zodiac Signs. Female planets in female signs and male planets in male signs get this source of strength. A male planet in a female sign or a female planet in a male sign do not derive this strength. Maximum strength - 30 virupas

4. **Kendradi Bala** - The 1, 4, 7, and 10 bhaavs or houses are collectively known as Kendra. The 2nd, 5th, 8th, and 11th are known as Succedent or panapara. The 3rd, 6th, 9th, and 12th are known as precedent houses or apoklima. Planets in the Kendra are the strongest, and those in the apoklima are the weakest. The planets placed in the panapara houses are of middling strength. Maximum strength - 60 virupas

5. **Drekkana Bala** - The male planets, namely Sun, Mars, and Jupiter, get their full strength in the 1st drekkana (the house of the sign itself). The female planets, namely Moon and Venus, get their full strength in the 2nd Drekkana (5th house from the Rashi). The eunuch planets, namely Mercury and Mars, get their full strength in the 3rd drekkana (the 9th house) of a Rashi or house. Maximum strength - 15 virupas.

From the above discussion, it is clear that if a planet achieves the maximum Saptavargaja bala, then the quantum of other Sthana bala becomes insignificant.

Dik Bala - the Directional Strength

This type of planetary strength is derived from the four Kendras, which represent the four directions or Dik. Lagna represents the East. Jupiter and Mercury get their Dik bala here. The 7th house from Lagna represents the West. Shani gets dik bala in this house. The 10th house represents the South. Mars and Sun get their dik bala in the 10th house. The 4th house represents the North where the Moon and Venus get their dik bala.

And the elements or tattva ruling the Lagna are the Akasha (ether) and Prithvi (earth). The element ruling the 4th house is Jala (water), that ruling the 7th house is Vayu (wind), and that ruling the 10th house is Agni (fire). When planets are in their dik balas, then the tattva lording over these houses also gets great prominence and strength, resulting in the native being blessed by the tattva devata.

Kala Bala - the Time Strength

This type of planetary strength depends on the time, such as hours, day, night, fortnight, month, year, etc. Each planet is strong at points in time and weak at other times. The maximum strength that can be achieved through Kala bala is 390 virupas. There are five components to Kala bala, including:

1. Natonnata Bala - This type of strength is based on day or night. Some planets are strong at night, and some are strong during the day. Sun, Jupiter, and Venus are strongest at noon. Moon, Mars, and Shani are strongest at midnight. Mercury is strong right through the day. Maximum strength - 60 virupas

2. Tribhaga Bala - In this type, day and night are each divided into 3 parts. Then, six planets (excluding Jupiter) get their maximum strength at different portions of day and night. Mercury, Sun, and Saturn are strong in the first, second, and third positions of the day, respectively. Moon, Venus, and Mars are strong in the first, second, and third portions of the night, respectively. Jupiter is strong through all the six portions. Maximum strength - 60 virupas

3. Paksha Bala - Some planets are strong during Krishna Paksha, while others are strong during Shukla Paksha. The benefic planets or shubh Grahas Chandra, Mercury, Jupiter, and Venus are strongest during Poornima. The malefic planets are strongest during Amavasya. Maximum strength - 60 virupas.

4. Varsha-Maas-Dina-Hora Bala - Different planets rule various time segments. It starts with the ruler of the year (Abda - solar year), which is subdivided into four components, namely month (Maas - solar month), week (Vara or Dina - Vedic weekday), and hour (hora - graha hour). Each of these four components is stronger than the previous one by 25%, making the Hora lord the strongest of the four. Vara Lord, which is the second strongest, is the Hora Lord at sunrise. Masa Lord, the third strongest, is the Hora Lord during the transit of the Sun from one Zodiac sign to the next. Abda Lord, the weakest of the four components, is the Hora Lord now when the Sun enters Aries. - Maximum strength - 150 virupas.

5. Ayana Bala - This source of Kala Bala depends on the movements of the planets in the Uttarayana or Dakshinayana directions. Maximum strength - 60 virupas.

Chesta Bala - Strength from the Motion of Planets

Chesta in Sanskrit translates to "effort", and the source of Chesta bala is determined by the efforts or movements made by planets. A planet that moves steadily is considered making fewer efforts, and when moving in retrograde, it is considered making a maximum effort. A retrograde movement can be compared to the movement against a flowing current, which requires a lot of effort.

The Sun and Moon always move steadily with no acceleration or retrogression. For planets Mercury to Saturn, Chesta Bala is calculated on the direction and speed of their movements. Calculating the Chest Bala of a planet uses a complex mathematical computation. There are eight different movements and their strengths defined in Vedic Astrology.

1. Vakra - Moving in reverse or retrogression - 100% strength, a planet's full brilliance is demonstrated at this strength.

2. Anuvakra - Moving to the previous Rashi when in retrogression - 60% strength

3. Vikala - No movement; the planet is standing still - 15% strength

4. Manda - Slow-moving, decelerating planet - 30% strength

5. Mandatara - Moving very slowly and appearing as if not moving at all - 15% strength

6. Sama - Slow acceleration - 7.5% strength

7. Chara - Moving in the forward direction at average speed - 45% strength

8. Atichara - Moving in the forward direction with above-average speed - 30% strength

Naisargika Bala - the Natural Strength

The natural strength of planets is called *Naisargika Bala*. Planets get progressively stronger in the following list:

- Saturn
- Mars
- Mercury
- Jupiter
- Venus
- Moon
- Sun

When two planets are positioned to mutually influence each other, then the stronger planet influences the weaker ones and predominantly produces its effects. From the above list, the Sun is the strongest planet. When any planet is in conjunction with the Sun, then it becomes combust. The Naisargika Bala of the Sun, while in conjunction with other planets, will never reduce.

Drgbala - the Aspect Strength

Drgbala is derived from being the natural aspect of the planet, whether naturally malefic or benefic. The aspect of natural malefic reduces the strength of the planet, while the aspect of natural benefic enhances its strength. The aspect's strength depends on the longitudinal difference between the aspected planet and the aspecting planet.

A naturally benefic planet (Venus, Jupiter, benefic Buddha, and the waxing Moon) aspects another planet, then it enhances the strength of the aspected planet. Contrarily, when naturally malefic planets (Mars, Saturn, Surya, Malefic Mercury, and the waning Moon) aspect a planet, then the aspected planet's strength is reduced.

Again, computing the Drgbala of a planet is complex and time-consuming. Most astrologers use a commonly accepted approximation method, which does cause a small error that can be ignored.

While it might be impractical to arrive at the strength of a planet mathematically (considering the complex computation usually involved), it is possible to arrive at accurate predictions based on understanding the conditions that render planets power. It is not necessary to know the complete, complex computation processes to know the strength and the corresponding effects of a planet. A proper understanding of the six-fold strength concept is sufficient. At this juncture, it makes sense to speak about Chandra's special power or strength, the Moon, considering this planet is seen as the natural sustainer and nurturer of a horoscope. The waxing and waning period of the Moon also affects its strength.

For Chandra, Paksha Bala is more important than Sthana Bala. Therefore, even if Chandra occupies a place that weakens its strength, but is strong because of Paksha Bala, then Chandra is considered strong. And if Chandra is placed in a strong position in a horoscope, the other planets' strength gets positively affected, as the Moon lends its power to the others. All the benefic planets acquire their strength during Chandra's Shukla Paksha. So, the more strength Chandra has in its Paksha Bala, the more power the benefic planets get.

Chapter 11: Timing of Events: Dashas and Transits

Astrology is all about timing future events and making accurate predictions. The Rashi Chart or birth chart of a native gives you an insight into the inherent promise held in his or her life based on the positions of the planets and other considerations connected to the planets, Rashis, etc. It only shows you the inherent promise that the life of the concerned native holds. But, when this promise can turn to fruition depends on elements called Dashas and the movement/transits of planets.

You have read and learned about the Dasa period of each planet. The total Dasa period of a planet or Graha is divided into multiple parts, which are, in turn, ruled by different planets and their lords. The Dasa that is operative, and the corresponding results involve various factors, including the natural signification of the planet, its ruler, its position and placement, aspects, and the strength.

The Dasa's major period is called the *mahadasha*, subdivided into smaller periods in which all the nine planets are operative within the mahadasha of a planet. The transit of planets, especially Shani and Guru, plays a crucial role in any important event happening in the lifetime of a native.

For example, Shani Mahadasha will have antardashas (sub-periods) within its 19-year duration. For instance, Shukra will be an antardasha within the Shani Mahadasha for 2 years and 9 months. So, during this period, the effects of Shani Mahadasha, along with Venus antardasha, should be analyzed for accurate predictions. During the 2years 9 months period of Venus antardasha, you must know what both Shani and Venus are doing in the Zodiac sky.

The promise when the effects of good karma fructify will depend on the Dasa and the planets' transit through the Dasa. Let us discuss important events that can be accurately predicted based on the birth chart, Dasas, and planets' transit. We will use examples to learn about the topics of this chapter.

Case Study I

Date of Birth - 13th December 1956; Time of Birth - 11:10 pm; Place of Birth - Delhi

When this person was born, the balance of Ketu Dasa happening at the time (calculated from the time of the native's birth) was 3 years, 11 months, and 1 day. Using this information, the Vimshottari Dasa of a person born on the above date, time, and place will be:

- Ketu Dasa (Balance remaining) - up to four years of age
- Shukra Dasa (20 years) - From 4 years up to 24 years of age
- Surya Dasa (six years) - from 24 years to 30 years of age
- Chandra Dasa (ten years) - from 30 years to 40 years of age

- Mangala Dasa (seven years) - from 40 years to 47 years of age

- Rahu Dasa (18 years) - from 47 to 65 years of age

- Guru Dasa (16 years) - from 65 to 81 years of age

- Shani Dasa (19 years) - from 81 to 100 years of age

Vimshottari Dasa affects the lifetime of a native as follows:

- During childhood - parents and the health of natives

- During adolescence or teenage - education

- During youth - mind, job, and family

- During old age - health, children, and caretaker of the native

For the above example, Ketu Dasa happened until he or she was 4 years old. Ketu was in the house of Shukra in Kendra, which represents father. Hence, this child's birth was good in terms of his or her health and the progress of the native's father.

From 4 years of age onwards, the native was influenced by Shukra Dasa. This period affects education. Shukra is in its own house, which is also the house of writing and artistic nature. The house of education is the fourth house occupied by Surya, Shani, and Rahu for this native. Rahu and Shani result in the child being thoughtful and introverted while Shani also renders interest in science. Buddha in the 5th house results in building the native's interesting in calculations. Therefore, the native would have likely been educated with a deep interest in science and mathematics.

From 24 to 30 years of age, Surya Dasa influenced this native. Surya, in this native's birth chart, is in the 4th house giving the individual the push needed to start his or her own business and earning a lot of fame at a young age. Chandra, the lord of the 12th house, brought luck and good fortune, resulting in good success in business for the native.

From 40 to 47 years, this native was influenced by Mangala Dasa. Even though Mars is a benefic planet, for this native, it is positioned in the 8th house, which results in a big setback to his profession and business.

Rahu Dasa for this person is the next. This planet is in debilitation but is in Kendra, and likely to have had good fortune. However, health problems could have come up during the Rahu Dasa for the native.

Guru Dasa sets in only at 62 years for this native, and it might be the best years of his or her life. The native is likely to lead a restful, serene life during Guru Dasa.

Transit of Planets

Usually, to study the transit of planets, only Shani, Guru, and Rahu are considered. This is because other planets move fast. Surya, Buddha, and Shukra rotate once a year, Mangala takes two years, Chandra takes just a month, and Ketu is always opposite to Rahu. So, it is enough to see only Shani (Saturn, which takes 30 years to complete one cycle), Rahu (which takes 18 years to complete one cycle), and Guru (which takes 12 years to complete one cycle) to study the transit of planets.

When a planet transits through the debilitation signs or the signs owned by its enemies, it will not give good, auspicious results. For example, when Saturn transits through Leo, Cancer, Scorpio, and Aries (also the sign of debilitation), which are owned by its enemies, it will combust and cannot reflect its full potential for about 25 days every year during the 19-year Mahadasha.

For Shukra, this inauspicious transits will happen when it passes through Cancer and Leo, both ruled by Venus' enemies. During its own mahadasha, it will combust once in a year for about 20 days. Also, these transits become very important during the Saturn-Venus sub-period of 2 years and 9 months.

When the owner of a Dasa or time period is in its sign of exaltation, its own sign, or in the signs of friendly planets, then the concerned Graha will give auspicious effects. In such circumstances, even during retrogressions, these planets do not give bad effects, and they could give auspicious effects.

For example, in Shani mahadasha, when Saturn transits through Capricorn, Aquarius, Virgo, Gemini, Libra, and Taurus, which are all exalted signs for the planet, then it will retrograde annually for about three to four months.

For Shukra mahadasha, this will happen when the planet transits through Gemini. Libra, Virgo, Aquarius, Pisces, and Capricorn. The duration of retrograde will be for about three to four months once a year.

Transits of planets are especially significant when they are in conjunction with the Moon. When Saturn crosses over the Moon, it is called *Sade Sati.* The native is likely to face big losses or progresses, depending on which sign the Moon is in. In the same way, Saturn passing through the 8th house from the Moon also results in tensions and losses.

In the above example, Guru crossed over Rahu/Shani when the native was 2, 14, 26, 28, 50, and 62 years of age. Saturn and Jupiter were in conjunction when the native was 12, 24, 36, 48, and 60 years of age. At the time of these transits, Jupiter was over the 4th house over Shani and Rahu, resulting in a change of residence or purchase of a new property. When Jupiter transited over the 7th house lorded by Saturn, then the native got married. Saturn over Saturn or Rahu resulted in losing business.

Also, the native experienced Sade Sati in 1968 and again in 1996. In 1968, the native lost academic interest, and in 1996, the native's mother fell ill, and there was a death in the family. Short transits show their results more prominently and effectively than mahadasha and antardashas. Yet, major transits affect the native in a big way. Shani transit over Chandra is very important. Guru and

Rahu transiting through the Lagna and the Moon give equal results. Typically, superimposing Dasas over the transit of planets gives more accurate predictions than otherwise.

Besides the Vimshottari Dasha System, the Yogini Dasha System is also used to calculate Dasas and transits of planets. It is important to realize the extreme difficulty of making accurate predictions in Vedic Astrology. There are multiple factors to be considered, each of which has its own rules and regulations for computations and mathematical analysis.

Dasas, transits of planets, divisional charts, planetary strengths, avasthas, and many more determinants are to be considered before accurate predictions can be arrived at. Even helped by computational software, the process of predictions for just one native can take a few hours, or perhaps, more.

Chapter 12: Ashtakavarga: Destiny Dots at a Glance

This final chapter in this of Vedic Astrology deals with Ashtakavarga or the eight-fold point system used to make predictions by just glancing at a horoscope. Although this tool is an independent subject, using it with the other tools mentioned in the previous chapters of this book can be a powerful predictive approach. Let us look at how this technique helps.

Sage Parashara also mentions the significance of this technique, used not only to determine the beneficial effects of planets through the Chandra and the ascendant but also to discover the auspiciousness of the houses by studying the transits of planets. The Ashtakavarga technique employs Bindu (dots) and Rekha (lines) to determine planets' position. This powerful tool is considered while analyzing mahadashas and antardashas of planets.

The Ashtakavarga table has multiple rows and columns. The top row is for the 12 Zodiac signs from Aries up to Pisces. The first right column is the ascendant's degree, and the first left column has the seven planets. Rahu and Ketu do not feature in the Ashtakavarga table. Instead, the Lagna itself is treated as a complete planet. The row against each planet represents the planet's score in the Zodiac sign of the respective column head. The last row is the combined score of each sign regarding the eight planets (including the Lagna). The last column is the combined score of each planet regarding the 12 signs.

In the Ashtakavarga table, the score of each planet-Zodiac sign combination varies from 0 to 8. Each planet's total score regarding the 12 Zodiac signs can range from 0 to 56. Only rules must interpret any Ashtakavarga table. Here are the two rules:

Rule #1 - Look at the row of each planet. You will notice that for every one of the 12 signs, the planet under consideration gets a score running from 0 to 8. Each point is an indicator of the planet's power to influence the sign related to the score. Here are the sub-rules related to Rule #1:

> • If the planet is in a sign where its score is between five and eight, then the planet will give auspicious results.

> • If the planet-sign combination score is four, then the results will be average.

> • If the planet-sign score is between zero and three, then it will give inauspicious results.

Rule #2 - Next, look at the individual sign totals, which is the last row of the table. The values in this row will range from 0 to 56. This row represents the power of each Zodiac sign to give related to its relationship with the planet position. Follow these guidelines to interpret the numerical values of this last row:

> • A Zodiac sign with a score of over 30 typically gives good results.

> • A sign with a total score of less than 25 means it is inauspicious.

> • Signs with scores between 25 and 80 give average results.

The following information can be obtained from an Ashtakavarga table:

- Weakest house - that house that has the lowest score
- Weak houses - those that have less than 25 points
- Average houses - those with a score between 25 and 30
- Strong houses - those with the highest scores or above 30

It is also important to know what the total score of all the 12 signs put together should be 337. If this number is different, then something has gone wrong in the table. Recheck it before moving on and trying to interpret it.

How to Use the Ashtakavarga Table for Rashi Chart Interpretation

First, mark the Lagna. Then mark the lowest and highest numerical value in the chart. Note down the house and Rashis these two numbers correspond to. Suppose the lowest number is in the 5th house, then start your analysis by investigating the 5th house, which primarily deals with children. While a problem with adolescents is indicated, it need not be a significant issue. The lowest number is only an indication for you or your astrologer to conduct a more detailed investigation in that particular house. As you dig deep, the depth and significance of the problem will become clear.

Similarly, if the lowest score is in the 9th house, it makes sense to investigate there. The 9th house deals with several important aspects of a native's life. But the most important factor of the 9th house is about the father or the head of the family. So, a low score here could mean that the native's father may have died at an early age or had health issues.

Another relevant point to note about Ashtakavarga charts is that they should not be used by themselves or separately to make predictions. It is critical to check other astrology factors, including the pertinent divisional charts, planetary strengths, etc. to interpret a native's life and life experiences correctly. But this table can be a powerful indicator of where to begin the investigation and find answers to other questions likely to arise as you verify various angles of a native's horoscope.

Here are more points about the Ashtakavarga table that will help you make good predictions:

If the number in the first house or Lagna is low and is also less than 25, then it means the native needs other people's support to do his or her work. This individual cannot do his or her karma by himself or herself. Such individuals always need somebody with them and cannot survive without a partner.

If the first house has a high score, then such people enjoy working alone. Such individuals are likely to have high egos, although they can make correct decisions with little help from others. People with a high score in the Lagna generally succeed, provided the other planetary positions are promising.

If the 12th house score is low, such individuals also have a good life because opportunities for loss and suffering are likely to be few. If the 12th score is the lowest, then such individuals are misers. They either don't have the mindset or the opportunity to spend money.

If the score of your 11th house (house of gains) is greater than that of your 12th house (house of loss), then too, it is good because it means you will gain more than you lose. If the condition is reversed, that is to say, the score in your 12th house is greater than that of your 11th house, then you are likely to spend more than you gain or earn.

Case Study of Ashtakavarga Table Scores

Let us take these scores of an Ashtakavarga table:

1st house - 25, 2nd house - 28, 3rd house - 33, 4th house - 29, 5th house - 26, 6th house - 24, 7th house - 35, 8th house - 35, 9th house - 26, 10th house - 27, 11th house - 22, and 12th house - 27. If you notice, the total score is 337. Let's interpret these scores:

- The average score is 337/12 = 28, which is also taken as a threshold. So, less than 28 is a bad score, and over 28 is a good score. This is the reason 25 to 30 is taken as average scores.

- In the above case study, the 1st, 5th, 6th, 9th, 10th, 11th, and 12th houses have scored less than 28. The 3rd, 4th, 7th, and 8th houses are of good value. The 2nd house with a value of 28 is average.

- Any house with a score of less than 25 is bad. Here, the 9th and the 11th houses are quite bad, the 11th being very bad. Values of the 1st, 9th, 10th, and 11th houses are also less than 30, which means they are negative indicators.

- The Lagna and the 4th houses also have less than 30.

- The value of 25 in the 1st house means that the native will boost his or her life after 25 years of age.

- The value of the 2nd house is 28, which is greater than the 11th and 12th houses' values. This means that the native will not waste their earnings and money.

- But the value of his 12th house is greater than the value of his 11th house, which means the native cannot hold on to his savings/earnings. This person's expenditure will be more than his or her income/earnings/savings.

Houses 1, 5, and 9 represent Bandhu, and the total for this native is 77

Houses 2, 6, and 10 represent Sevaka, and the total is 79

Houses 3, 7, and 11 represent Poshaka; the total value is 90

Houses 4, 8, and 12 represent Ghataka; the total value is 91

If the Bandhu group has the highest tally, then the native will have ample resources, will do good karma, and be charitable. If the Sevaka group has the highest tally, then the native will be in employment or service, and he or she will be money-minded. If the Poshaka group gets the highest tally, then the native may be an industrialist, employer, or a boss. If the Ghataka group has the highest tally, then the native could be very poor.

It takes time and effort to understand and interpret the Ashtakavarga table. But, when used with the other astrological tools and techniques mentioned in this book, it can be a powerfully accurate predictor of horoscopes.

Conclusion

At first glance, Vedic Astrology might appear confounding to the novice. It is easy to relate to this feeling of being overwhelmed by the information this engrossing and captivating subject covers. Yes, it does take a bit of effort on your part to understand the concepts of Jyotishya.

But you can rest assured that your efforts will not be in vain. With sustained and persistent practice and reading, you will learn to look at a horoscope or table, use quick computations, and gauge what lies in store for the native.

Knowing Jyotishya is useful for your own life. When you achieve great success, you can review your own horoscope and know that you are not doing this on your own. You will learn that your past karmas are giving you beneficial outcomes. When you suffer a lot, again, simply reading your horoscope will give you an insight as to how long you must endure the difficult times.

Viewing the happy and sad parts of your life with equanimity will keep you grounded and empower you to give your best shot to everything you try. For such individuals, successes will far outnumber the failures. So, go ahead, and read the book again and again until you have mastered the basics. You can then move on to advanced levels.

Part 2: Nakshatras

The Ultimate Guide to the 27 Lunar Mansions of Vedic Astrology

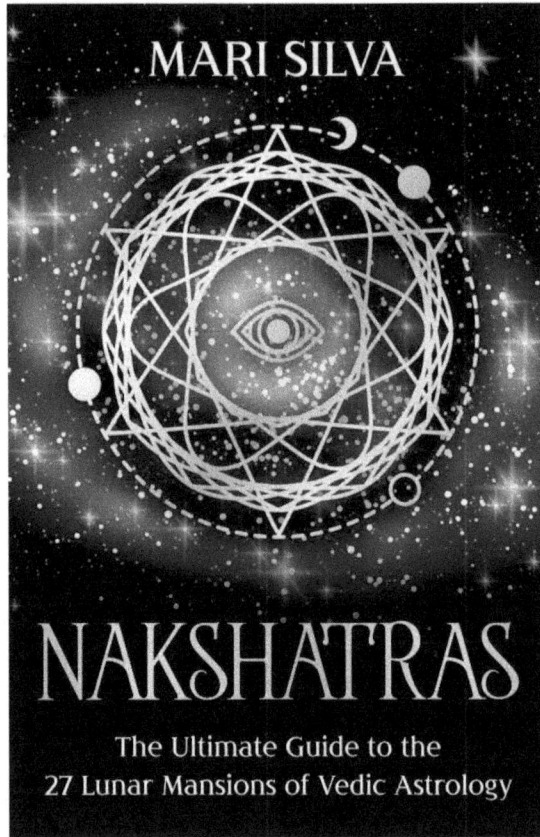

Introduction

Nakshatras are segments of the ecliptic through which the Moon passes on its orbit around the Earth. Otherwise known as lunar mansions, ancient cultures use them in their organization of the calendar. Simply put, Nakshatras are asterisms, constellations, or groups of stars that are fixed and immobile. Planets pass over them as they move in their orbits.

The ancient Indian sages who created the Vedic Astrology and Nakshatras system say these lunar mansions are the homes in which the fruits of labor—or karma, in Sanskrit—are stored. The stars of asterisms distribute karma in the present life.

Although more popular in Hindu Astrology, the concept of using stars of asterisms was adopted in other parts of the world, too, including the Euphrates Valley of Mesopotamia, Babylonia, Egypt, Arabia, and Person.

The history of the study of Nakshatras is not relevant in this book. More interesting is that by knowing about Nakshatras and their influences on your life, you can know where your life is going, and potentially, even find out why.

This comprehensive publication on Nakshatras extensively covers the basic aspects of this fascinating topic. While it may take years of learning and practice to master this idea, it has been written in simple, easy-to-understand language, and is great for beginners who want to test the waters.

The best part of the book is that it has all the latest trends in Nakshatras' realm, along with the updated tools used to arrive at predictions. The chapters have been arranged so you will learn the simplest topics first and develop into the progressively complex topics. It is best to start from the first topic to get an idea of each chapter before moving on to the next. By the time you finish the book, your understanding of Nakshatras and their effects on human life will have exceeded your original expectations.

SECTION ONE: The 27 Lunar Mansions

Chapter 1: Introduction to the 27 Lunar Mansions

Nakshatra is a Sanskrit term relating to a house (mansion) of the moon—astrologically referred to as a lunar mansion. The term Nakshatra is used both in Indian astronomy and in Hindu or Vedic Astrology. The moon's ecliptic orbit around the Earth is divided into 27 sectors, each of which is a Nakshatra. Each Nakshatra's name is connected to an important star or group of stars (asterism) in that sector.

According to Vedic Astrology, in Sanskrit, Nakshatra translates to "star," and the 27 Nakshatras play an undeniably important role in astrological calculations. As you may call it, the Zodiac—or the heavens—was categorized into twelve Rashis or Zodiac Signs. India's ancient seers used a more accurate and detailed categorization of the heavens into 27 Nakshatras or asterisms.

These 27 Nakshatras or constellations are about 300-400 light-years away from the Earth. Vedic Astrology offers detailed descriptions along with accurate mathematical and astronomical calculations by which a practitioner has a powerful predictive tool in their hand based on an individual's Nakshatra at their birth.

According to ancient Vedic astrology, the starting point of the 27 Nakshatras is "Kritika," or the vernal equinox's position. However, more recent compilations of Vedic Astrology take the starting point of the list of 27 Nakshatras as "Ashwini," a point on the ecliptic that is directly opposite to "Chitra," the Sanskrit name for the star Spica. "Ashwini" is the asterism connected to the modern constellation of Aries. The first Vedic Astrological text that lists these 27 Nakshatras is Vedanga Jyotisha.

The Hindu scriptures like the Mahabharata and Harivamsa credit the creation of the Nakshatras to Daksha, an important son of Lord Brahma, the universe's creator. The story of Daksha and how he is credited with creating the Nakshatra goes as follows:

Lord Brahma, the creator of the universe, created Daksha, Kamadeva, Dharma, and Agni from his right thumb, heart, chest, and eyebrows, respectively. Daksha is portrayed as a fat man with a protruding belly and an ibex's head with spiral horns. Daksha and his wife Prasuti had many daughters. He married 27 of them to Chandra, the Moon God.

Interestingly, Chandra was only keen on marrying one of Daksha's daughters, Rohini, but Daksha requested the Moon God to marry another 26, along with Rohini. Thus, the 27 wives of Chandra, the Moon God, became the 27 Nakshatras or Lunar Mansions.

In the Atharva Veda, one of the four Vedas in the Sanatana Dharma—now known in the Western world as Hinduism—talks about 28 Nakshatras, which are used as celestial markers in the sky. When these 28 stars were mapped into equal divisions of the ecliptic, it resulted in 27 divisions. Those represented 27 cleaner and more accurate segments, each subtending to 13° 20' (13 degrees 20 minutes) instead of 12° 5 1-3/7' (12 degrees and 1-3/7 minutes) in the earlier 28 sections.

The 27 stars according to Vedic Astrology are Ashwini, Bharani, Kritika, Rohini, Mrigashirsha, Ardra, Punarvasu, Pushya, Aslesha, Magha, Purva Phalguni, Uttara Phalguni, Hasta, Chitra, Swati, Vishakha, Anuradha, Jyeshtha, Moola, Purvashada, Uttarashada, Shravana, Dhanishta, Satabhisha, Purva Bhadrapada, Uttara Bhadrapada, and Revati.

The Nakshatra Abhijit was left out from the 28 listed in the Atharva Veda; however, rare astrological schools consider all 28 Nakshatras. Interestingly, this abandoned Nakshatra Abhijit plays an important role while deciding auspicious times to conduct important events in all schools of Vedic Astrology.

Relationship Between Nakshatras and Zodiac Signs

Understanding planetary rulers form a key element in Vedic Astrology. In ancient Hindu Astrology, only the five visible planets, namely Mercury, Venus, Mars, Jupiter, and Saturn, along with the Sun and Moon, are the rulers of the twelve Zodiac Signs covering the 27 Nakshatras. These seven heavenly bodies together are referred to as the "Traditional Rulers." The Sun and Moon rule one Zodiac sign each—Leo and Cancer, respectively—and the remaining five visible planets rule two signs each. In addition to the Traditional Rulers, Rahu and Ketu (Lunar Nodes) also rule certain Nakshatras.

Another important point to note is that Zodiac signs also have their own lords, taken from the nine rulers described above. Every Nakshatra is ruled by its own lord and gets influenced by the lord of the sign to which it belongs.

The above 27 Nakshatras start at Ashwini at 0 degrees, and each of the Nakshatras covers 13 degrees, 20 minutes in 360 degrees of the path. Further, each of these Nakshatras is divided into four quarters (Padas) measuring 3 degrees, 20 minutes. The twelve

Rashis covers 30 degrees each in the 360-degree path. The first Rashi or the Zodiac sign, namely Mesha—which covers 0-30 degrees—has ten padas of the first three Nakshatras as follows:

- All the four padas of the first Nakshatra, Ashwini (13 degrees, 20 minutes)
- All the four padas of the second Nakshatra, Bharani (13 degrees, 20 minutes)
- The first pada of the third Nakshatra, Kritika (3 degrees, 20 minutes)

So, the next Rashi, Vrishabh, will have the following Nakshatra padas covered in it:

- The second, third, and the fourth pada of third Nakshatra, Kritika (10 degrees)
- All the four padas of the fourth Nakshatra, Rohini (13 degrees, 20 minutes)
- The first and second padas of the fifth Nakshatra, Mrigasheersha (6 degrees, 40 minutes)

Like this, each of the twelve Rashis encloses nine padas from the various Nakshatras, taken in order.

Now, look at each of these Nakshatras in more detail.

The 27 Nakshatras

Ashwini - The Ashwini Nakshatra ranges from 0 degrees to 13 degrees, 20 minutes in the Mesha Rashi or the Aries sign. Ketu, the Serpent God, is the ruler of Ashwini Nakshatra. Ashwini is identified with the serpent god and also symbolizes all the serpentine qualities. Its symbol is the horse's head.

Bharani - The Bharani Nakshatra ranges between 13 degrees, 20 minutes, and 24 degrees, 40 minutes in the Mesha Rashi, or the Aries sign. The Lord Yama, the God of Death, is the ruler of the Bharani Nakshatra. Lord Yama is the dispenser of justice as he analyzes the good and bad actions and behaviors of a person, determining the punishment or reward for the person's soul after their death. The symbol of Bharani Nakshatra is the Yoni.

Kritika – The Kritika Nakshatra ranges from 26 degrees, 40 minutes from the Aries sign to 10 degrees in the Vrishabh Rashi or Taurus sign. The ruler of Kritika Nakshatra is the Sun God, Surya. People born in this Nakshatra are usually tenacious, determined, and have a strong will to get what they want. Its symbol is the razor.

Rohini – Rohini Nakshatra ranges from 10 degrees to 23 degrees, 20 minutes in the Vrishabh Rashi. The ruling planet of the Rohini Nakshatra is Chandra, the Moon. This star focuses on spiritual liberation and the idea that desiring anything that is not yours is not a good thing. It symbolizes a chariot and is also referred to as the "Red One." Its symbol is the chariot.

Mrigashirsha – The Mrigashirsha Nakshatra ranges from 23 degrees, 20 minutes in the Vrishabh Rashi to 6 degrees, 40 minutes in Mithuna Rashi, or Gemini Zodiac sign. Mrigashirsha translates to "deer's head" and symbolizes benevolence. The ruling planet is Mars, and its symbol is the deer's head.

Ardra – The Ardra Nakshatra ranges from 6 degrees, 40 minutes to 20 degrees in Mithuna Rashi. It is ruled by Lord Rudra, the manifestation of power and dominance, as well as Rahu, the shadow planet, which can bring many miseries, including sadness and poverty. Its symbol is a teardrop.

Punarvasu – Ranging from 20 degrees in Mithuna Rashi to 3 degrees, 20 minutes in Karka Rashi (the Cancer zodiac sign), Punarvasu means the return of light. The ruling planet is Jupiter, and people born under this Nakshatra are known for their never-give-up attitude. They can stand up and fight regardless of the number of times they are beaten. Its symbol is a quiver.

Pushya – The Pushya Nakshatra ranges from 3 degrees, 20 minutes to 16 degrees, 40 minutes in the Karka Rashi. The Lord of this Nakshatra is Saturn, and natives of Pushya are usually happy, rich, good-looking, stable-minded, and have self-esteem. Its symbol is the udder.

Aslesha – The Ashlesha Nakshatra ranges from 16 degrees, 40 minutes to 30 degrees in Karka Rashi, and is ruled by the Serpent God. Ashlesha translates to "Naga," or the serpent deity, and represents snake-like qualities such as entwining, embracing, and clinging. Its symbol is a serpent.

Magha – The Magha Nakshatra ranges from 0 degrees to 13 degrees, 20 minutes in the Simha Rashi (the Zodiac Sign of Leo). The natives born in Magha Nakshatra are usually attracted to occult sciences and are prone to invoking and praying to their ancestors. Ketu rules this Nakshatra, and its symbol is a throne.

Purva Phalguni – The Purva Phalguni Nakshatra ranges from 13 degrees, 20 minutes to 26 degrees, 40 minutes in the Simha Rashi, and is ruled by the planet Venus. Natives born in this Nakshatra usually love to enjoy materialistic comforts. Its symbol is a hammock.

Uttara Phalguni – The Uttara Phalguni Nakshatra ranges from 26 degrees, 40 minutes in the Simha Rashi to 10 degrees in Kanya Rashi (Virgo zodiac sign). The ruler of Uttara Phalguni is Surya, the Sun God. Natives born under this Nakshatra are usually friendly and independent. Its symbol is a fig tree.

Hasta – The Hasta Nakshatra ranges from 10 degrees to 23 degrees, 20 minutes in Kanya Rashi. The Lord of Hasta Nakshatra is Chandra, the Moon God. People born in this Nakshatra are typically pure in thought, word, and deed. Its symbol is the hand.

Chitra - The Chitra Nakshatra ranges from 23 degrees, 20 minutes in the Kanya Rashi, and goes up to 6 degrees, 40 minutes in Tula Rashi (Libra zodiac sign). The planet Mars rules the Chitra Nakshatra. Its symbol is a jewel.

Swati - Ranging from 6 degrees, 40 minutes to 20 degrees in Tula Rashi, Swati Nakshatra is ruled by Rahu, the shadow planet. People born in Swati Nakshatra are usually skilled at their profession, compassion, soft-spoken, and generous. Its symbol is coral.

Vishakha - The Vishakha Nakshatra ranges from 20 degrees in Tula Rashi to 3 degrees, 20 minutes in Vrischika Rashi (Scorpio). Ruled by the planet Jupiter, the natives born in Vishakha Nakshatra are usually adept at making money. Its symbol is an arch.

Anuradha - The Anuradha Nakshatra ranges from 3 degrees, 20 minutes to 16 degrees, 40 minutes in Vrischika Rashi. Interestingly, Vrischika Rashi is ruled by the aggressive planet Mars, and Saturn rules the Anuradha Nakshatra. Now, Mars and Saturn are considered rivals with characteristics that are starkly different from each other. So, people born in Anuradha Nakshatra demonstrate peculiar traits. Its symbol is a lotus.

Jyeshtha - The Jyeshtha Nakshatra ranges from 16 degrees, 40 minutes to 30 degrees in Vrischika Rashi. The ruling lord of this Nakshatra is the planet Mercury. People born under this Nakshatra have excellent analytical skills, are virtuous and cheerful, but have very few friends. Its symbol is an amulet.

Moola - The Moola Nakshatra ranges from 0 degrees to 13 degrees, 20 minutes in Dhanush Rashi (Sagittarius). The controlling planet of Moola is Ketu. Roots are the symbol of this constellation.

Purvashada – The Purvashada Nakshatra ranges from 13 degrees, 20 minutes to 26 degrees, 40 minutes in Dhanush Rashi. People born in this Nakshatra are usually very proud, compatible with their partners, and are attached to their friends. The ruling planet is planet Venus, and the symbol is a fan.

Uttarashada – The Uttarashada Nakshatra ranges from 13 degrees, 20 minutes in the Dhanush Rashi to 10 degrees in Makar Rashi (Capricorn). The ruling Lord of this Nakshatra is Surya or the Sun. People born in this Nakshatra are usually grateful, obedient, and spiritual seekers. Its symbol is the tusk.

Shravana – The Shravana Nakshatra ranges from 10 degrees to 23 degrees, 20 minutes in Makar Rashi. It is ruled by the Moon or Chandra. People born in this Nakshatra are usually seekers of knowledge and wisdom. Its symbol is an ear.

Dhanishta – Ruled by Mars, the Dhanishta Nakshatra ranges from 23 degrees, 20 minutes in Makar Rashi to 6 degrees, 40 minutes in Kumbha Rashi (Aquarius). The ruling god is Saturn. People born in this Nakshatra are usually versatile and intelligent. Its symbol is a drum.

Satabhisha – The Satabhisha Nakshatra ranges from 6 degrees, 40 minutes to 20 degrees in Kumbha Rashi. The ruling planet is Rahu. People born in this Nakshatra are truthful and honest, even though they talk harshly. Its symbol is a collection of 1,000 stars.

Purva Bhadrapada – The Purva Bhadrapada Nakshatra ranges from 20 degrees in Kumbha Rashi to 3 degrees, 20 minutes in Meena Rashi (Pisces). The ruling planet is Jupiter. People born in this Nakshatra are usually intelligent and adept at making money. Its symbol is a funeral cot.

Uttara Bhadrapada – Ranging from 3 degrees, 20 minutes to 16 degrees, 40 minutes in Meena Rashi, the Uttara Bhadrapada Nakshatra is ruled by Saturn. People born under this Nakshatra are usually happy, love children, and have good oratory skills. Its symbol is a water snake.

Revati – The Revati Nakshatra ranges from 16 degrees, 40 minutes to 30 degrees in Meena Rashi. The ruling planet is Mercury. People born under this Nakshatra are usually amicable, knowledgeable, and wealthy. Its symbol is a fish.

Categorizations of the 27 Nakshatras

The 27 Nakshatras are categorized into different types based on their favorability for auspicious times of various events.

Sthira or Fixed – There are four Nakshatras, namely Rohini, Uttara Phalguni, Uttara Ashadha, and Uttara Bhadrapada, referred to as fixed or sthira. Sthira translates to stable, and so, these asterisms are excellent for activities with long-term effects and outcomes, such as tree planting, buying a home or other property, and construction of buildings.

Ugra or Fierce – The five constellations classified as fierce or ugra are Bharani, Magha, Purva Phalguni, Purva Ashadha, and Purva Bhadrapada. According to Hindu Astrology, these asterisms are excellent for activities involving fire, destruction, demolitions, weapons, handling of excessive force, confronting enemies and rivals, etc.

Chara or Movable – The five asterisms categorized as movable are Punarvasu, Swati, Shravana, Dhanishtha, and Shatabhisha. Chara translates to movability, and so these Nakshatras are ideal for activities connected to mobility and moving parts and items. Examples include the purchase of vehicles, going on journeys, or traveling.

Mridu or Tender – The four Nakshatras categorized as tender or mridu are Mrigashira, Chitra, Anuradha, and Revati. Due to their tender nature, these asterisms are suitable for seeking and enjoying pleasures and pleasurable activities. For example, they are good for writing poetry, making new friends, the beginnings of dramas, and dances.

Tikshna or Sharp – Four Nakshatras are categorized as sharp or tikshna, including Ardra, Ashlesha, Jyeshtha, and Mula. These asterisms' sharp nature renders them useful for difficult activities such as filing for divorce, black magic, casting spells, exorcism, and hypnotism.

Kshipra or Swift – There are three asterisms categorized as Kshipra or swift, namely Ashwini, Pushya, and Hasta. Their swift nature makes these Nakshatras highly suitable for finance, education, and trade-related activities. Thus, these constellations are suitable for trade and commerce transactions, admission to institutions, loan-related tasks, taking medication, and journey and travel.

Misra or Mixed – Two Nakshatras, namely Krittika and Vishaka, are called mixed or misra. Due to their mixed nature, these asterisms are good for routine activities such as worshipping, purchasing electronics and furniture, and fire ceremonies.

Chapter 2: A Closer Look at Nakshatras

Chapter 1 provided basic information about each Nakshatra. Chapter 2 takes a closer look at each of the 27 Nakshatras. However, before that, there are other preliminary and very important elements in Vedic Astrology that you need to be aware of.

The Three Gunas

Indian philosophy divides reality into two categories: Purusha, the knower, and Prakriti, the known. Purusha or the Self is never an experiential object; it is always the subject matter. Purusha is that which knows everything and is totally aware. On the other hand, Prakriti is all that shows itself, including material and psychological elements. Prakriti consists of everything that can be known.

Prakriti is a gigantic reservoir of limitless potential or energy made up of three primary forces or gunas, which include Sattva, Rajas, and Tamas. Each of these gunas has its own characteristics. Knowing how these three gunas work and understanding their essence is an important tool on the spiritual path. It also plays an important role in Vedic Astrology. Now, look at each of these three gunas—which translates to "strand" or "fiber"—in more detail.

Sattva - Sattva behaves like a transparent glass, allowing the light and knowledge of the pure consciousness to flow through easily. It has the power to unveil the ultimate truth—or Sat in Sanskrit. Sattva manifests through inspiration, beauty, and balance and promotes health, contentment, and energy. Sattva is the energy connected to liberation. It goes beyond the materialistic world and yearns to return to its original, heavenly abode.

Rajas - This fundamental force of Prakriti is related to change and is characterized by passion, effort, desire, and pain. The activity of Rajas can drive you toward Sattva (increased spirituality) or Tamas (increased desire for materialism). Although it can have positive or negative outcomes, Rajas is characterized by unsteadiness, agitation, and unhappiness.

Tamas - This fundamental force or energy layer of Prakriti hides the presence of Pure Consciousness. The power of Tamas to obscure results in dullness and ignorance. This fundamental force is heavy and dense. Interestingly, another synonym of Tamas is "sthithi," or being steady. Tamas, in a Sattvic form, can have a steadying influence in one's life. For example, resting during illness can be therapeutic.

Tamas is almost always characterized by immobilization. Therefore, tamasic foods are impure, stale, and lifeless. Tamasic entertainment is intoxicating and mindless. All things from Tamas invariably leads to inaction even when action is the need of the hour. The attraction to lethargy, sleep, and procrastination is a common tamasic effect that nearly everyone experiences. Tamas is all about the material world.

Nakshatras and the Three Gunas

Each of the 27 Nakshatras represents the three gunas in three different ways or levels. Now, look at each of the three levels to understand the connection between gunas and Nakshatras better.

First-Level Relationship – The 27 Nakshatras are divided into three categories, each with nine Nakshatras representing one of the three fundamental forces. Thus, at a primary level:

- Nine of the 27 Nakshatras representing Rajas energy coincide with the Zodiac Signs Aries, Taurus, Gemini, and Cancer.

- Another group of nine Nakshatras representing Tamas energy coincides with the Zodiac Signs Leo, Virgo, Libra, and Scorpio.

- The third group of nine Nakshatras representing Sattva energy coincides with the Zodiac signs Sagittarius, Capricorn, Aquarius, and Pisces.

Second-Level Relationship – Each group of nine Nakshatras is further divided into three groups of three Nakshatras, each at the secondary level. So, the nine Nakshatras representing Rajas energy at the primary level are divided as follows:

- The first three Nakshatras represent Rajas at the secondary level.

- The next three represent Tamas at the secondary level.

- The last three represent Sattva at the secondary level.

Similarly, the nine Nakshatras representing Tamas energy are divided into three groups as follows at the secondary level:

- The first three Nakshatras represent Rajas energy.

- The second three Nakshatras represent Tamas energy.

- The last three Nakshatras represent Sattva energy.

In the same way, the nine Nakshatras representing Sattva energy are divided into three groups as follows:

- The first three Nakshatras represent Rajas energy.

- The second three Nakshatras represent Tamas energy.

- The last three Nakshatras represent Sattva energy.

Tertiary-Level Relationship – Each of the three Nakshatras at the secondary level is further divided into three categories, each representing Rajas, Tamas, and Sattva energies. With this system, the 27 Nakshatras and the three fundamental energies interacting with each other along with their respective planetary lords are as follows:

1. Ashwini – Rajas-Rajas-Rajas – Ketu

2. Bharani – Rajas-Rajas-Tamas – Venus (or Shukra)

3. Krittika – Rajas-Rajas-Sattva – Sun (Surya)

4. Rohini – Rajas-Tamas-Rajas – Moon (Chandra)

5. Mrigashirsha – Rajas-Tamas-Tamas – Mars (Guja)

6. Ardra – Rajas-Tamas-Sattva – Rahu

7. Punarvasu – Rajas-Sattva-Rajas – Jupiter (Guru)

8. Pushya – Rajas-Sattva-Tamas – Saturn (Shani)

9. Ashlesha – Rajas-Sattva-Sattva – Mercury (Bhuddh)

10. Magha – Tamas-Rajas-Rajas – Ketu

11. Purva Phalguni – Tamas-Rajas-Tamas – Venus (Shukra)

12. Uttara Phalguni – Tamas-Rajas-Sattva – Sun (Surya)

13. Hasta – Tamas-Tamas-Rajas – Moon (Chandra)

14. Chitra – Tamas-Tamas-Tamas – Mars (Guja)

15. Swati – Tamas-Tamas-Sattva – Rahu

16. Vishakha – Tamas-Sattva-Rajas – Jupiter (Guru)

17. Anuradha – Tamas-Sattva-Tamas – Saturn (Shani)

18. Jyeshta – Tamas-Sattva-Sattva – Mercury (Buddh)

19. Mula – Sattva-Rajas-Rajas – Ketu

20. Purvashadha – Sattva-Rajas-Tamas – Venus (Shukra)

21. Uttarashadha – Sattva-Rajas-Sattva – Sun (Surya)

22. Shravana – Sattva-Tamas-Rajas – Moon (Chandra)

23. Dhanistha – Sattva-Tamas-Tamas – Mars (Guja)

24. Shatabhisha – Sattva-Tamas-Sattva – Rahu

25. Purva Bhadrapada – Sattva-Sattva-Rajas – Jupiter (Guru)

26. Uttara Bhadrapada – Sattva-Sattva-Tamas – Saturn (Shani)

27. Revati – Sattva-Sattva-Sattva – Mercury (Bhuddh)

Connection Between Lords of the Nakshatras and the Gunas

The lords of the Nakshatras play an important role in the life of a person. The lord of the Nakshatra, in which the Moon is placed at the time of a person's birth, determines the first "dasa" of the individual's life. Dasas and their importance will be detailed later. Interestingly, a critical connection can be found between the lords of the Nakshatras and the gunas.

- Ketu, Shukra, and Surya are the lords of those Nakshatras with Rajas at the secondary level.

- Chandra, Guja, and Rahu are the lords of the Nakshatras with Tamas at the secondary level.

- Guru, Shani, and Bhuddh are the lords of the Nakshatras with Sattva at the secondary level.

Now, look at the tertiary level.

- Shukra, Guja, and Shani are the lords of the Nakshatras that have Tamas at the tertiary level.

- Surya, Rahu, and Bhuddh are the Nakshatras lords with Sattva at the tertiary level.

- Ketu, Chandra, and Guru are the lords of those Nakshatras that have Rajas at the tertiary level.

Looking at the secondary and tertiary levels, you get the following information about the nine planets and the gunas.

- Ketu – Rajas-Rajas
- Shukra (Venus) – Rajas-Tamas
- Surya (Sun) – Rajas-Sattva
- Chandra (Moon) – Tamas-Rajas
- Guja (Mars) – Tamas-Tamas
- Rahu – Tamas-Sattva
- Guru (Jupiter) – Sattva-Rajas
- Shani (Saturn) – Sattva-Tamas
- Bhuddh (Mercury) – Sattva-Sattva

Now, you can draw some really fascinating connections between the planets and the gunas with examples.

- Venus (Shukra) is known for love and lust. To get love and lust, you take action (Rajas), and the deeper you get into action, the more you fall into ignorance (Tamas).

- Surya is a fiery (Rajas) planet, but it also represents the soul and has Sattva characteristics.

- Guru is also a fiery (Rajas) planet. However, again, Guru represents inner wisdom and is Sattvic.

- Saturn is a spiritual (Sattva) planet because it is related to Sannyas (renouncement). But Saturn also represents matter (or material), which is why it has Tamasic characteristics.

- Rahu is like Shani but in the reverse order. Rahu takes you so deep into materialistic life that you accept everything that this life has to give you and then follow the path of liberation (Sattva).

- Bhuddh (Mercury) comes across as the most spiritual planet—and the reason is clear. It is an airy planet and has the power to liberate you from suffering. Unlike animals, human beings can think for themselves. Mercury helps you do that. It is neither connected to Tamas (materialism) nor Rajas (activity). It merely thinks about these two without going into either of the two.

Padas and Navamsas

As you already know, every Nakshatra is divided into four padas of 3 degrees, 30 minutes each. A Navamsa chart is used to depict the padas of Nakshatras. Nav-amsa means the "nine parts" or divisions of a Zodiac Sign. Each Zodiac sign has nine padas in it, making it a total of 108 padas in the entire elliptic. A Navamsa chart is considered the most important divisional charts—or Varga charts—to make predictive readings of an individual's life.

It has to be read in conjunction with the fundamental natal—or Rashi—chart. If the natal chart is compared to a blueprint, the Navamsa chart shows what that blueprint can become. Every pada is expressed through one of the twelve Navamsa signs and the ruling lord of that particular sign. Every pada alternates with male and female expressions, as do the twelve Zodiac Signs. Padas are discussed further in the next chapter.

The 27 Nakshatras and their Dileanations

Now, look at each of the 27 Nakshatras in more detail.

Ashwini - The Ashwini Nakshatra represents the Ashwini Kumara twins named Castor and Pullox. Spanning from 0 degrees to13 degrees, 20 minutes in Aries or Mesha Rashi, Ashwini's ruling planet is Ketu. The element connected to Ashwini is earth, and its symbol is the head of a horse.

The Ashwini Kumaras, the physicians to the gods or devas, rule over this constellation. This constellation can help people be free of diseases and deliver miraculous cures. People born in this Nakshatra are usually popular, good-looking, skillful, intelligent, and love all decorative elements.

The character of Ashwini Nakshatra is light and swift and is good for undertaking journeys, starting treatments, beginning a study course, making and manufacturing jewelry, and enjoying luxurious items.

Bharani - The ruler of Bharani is Lord Yama, the god of death, who has the power to take things away—referred to as apabharani shakti. So, Bharani Nakshatra takes away those things that have completed their life term on Earth and moves them to the next world. Lord Yama takes the soul of the person who has completed their life on Earth and takes it to the astral plane, where the soul can experience the effects of its karma of the present world and prepare itself for the next world or birth.

Lord Yama stands for discipline, sacrifice, cleanliness, purity, integrity, and justice. The Nakshatra, over which this lord rules also, is a giver of what is good, truthful, pure, and honest. Bharani Nakshatra's astrological nature is fierce and cruel. It is suitable for getting jobs done immediately, competitions, cruel deeds, and tasks related to poison, fire, and dangerous chemicals. Bharani Nakshatra is not suitable to start any auspicious events or work.

Bharani is connected to the earth element, and Shukra is the ruler of this constellation. Natives of Bharani Nakshatra are usually successful in their professions, truthful, and are free from grief. They will have a resolute character and no health issues.

Krittika – The first pada falls in Mesha Rashi while the remaining three padas fall in the Vrishabha Rashi. The ruling lord of Krittika is Agni, and the ruling planet is Surya. The element of Krittika is the earth, and the symbol is a goat. People born in the Krittika Nakshatra are usually attractive, voracious eaters, famous, and known to have a roving eye.

The lord of this Nakshatra is Agni, who has the power to burn, referred to as dahana shakti. The nature of Agni is to give light and heat, which are important elements for purification. So, the power of Krittika Nakshatra can burn up negativity, purifies a mixture of positive and negative, and can cook or ripen uncooked and raw things.

Krittika Nakshatra's nature is of mixed quality. It is an auspicious star for doing immediate actions, to start competitions, to work with metals, and to start an argument, but it is not an auspicious star to begin long-term, important tasks.

Rohini – All the four padas of Rohini Nakshatra are in Vrishabha Rashi. Derived from the Sanskrit root, Rohan meaning rising or coming into existence, Rohini is the birth star of Lord Krishna. According to Hindu mythology, Rohini was one of Chandra's 27 wives, the one he loved the most. Chandra rules Rohini, and the symbol is a cow-drawn cart.

Natives of Rohini Nakshatra are usually truthful, do not covet others' properties, speak sweetly, have clean habits, good-looking, and have firm views. The lord of Rohini Nakshatra is Lord Brahma, the creator, whose power is to create or grow, referred to as rohana shakti. Rohini Nakshatra's power lies in its ability to make anything fertile and allow for growth and development.

People born in Rohini Nakshatra—who invariably live well and abundantly—are also prone to jealous attacks from others. Yet, these are only side effects of the power of achieving great prosperity.

Being a steady and fixed Nakshatra, Rohini is auspicious for laying the foundations for cities, towns, digging wells, planting trees, coronations, building temples, installing deities, and other such activities that have lasting effects.

Mrigashirsha – The first and second padas of Mrigashirsha is in Vrishabha Rashi, and the third and fourth padas are in Mithuna Rashi. The ruling planet of this Nakshatra is Mangala or Mars, and the ruling lord is Chandra. The symbol of Mrigashirsha is the antelope.

People born in Mrigashirsha Nakshatra are usually skillful, good speakers, knowledgeable, and rich, but also cowardly and capricious. They are quite timid and peace-loving. The lord of Mrigashirsha is Chandra, also called Soma—the nectar of immortality)—the Moon God. Soma renders prana Shakti—or fulfillment. Chandra in Mrigashirsha also stands for weaving and expansion. So, Mrigashirsha Nakshatra has the power to fill their lives and those of others with joy and fulfillment.

Mrigashirsa is an auspicious star for accepting initiation, weddings, building constructions, and undertaking journeys. It has a gentle and soft nature and is good for learning arts, sensual pleasures, wearing new clothes, festivities, and other joyful events.

Ardra – All the four padas of Ardra Nakshatra are in Mithuna Rashi. The ruling lord of this Nakshatra is Rudra—a form of Lord Shiva—the trident and bow wielder. Ardra is the Janma Nakshatra of Lord Shiva. The ruling planet is Rahu, and the symbol is a teardrop.

Natives born under the Ardra Nakshatra are typically skillful traders and are highly interested in Tantric rituals. On the flip side, these natives can be quite ungrateful, have a fierce temper, and indulge in wicked deeds.

Lord Rudra represents thunder and is the fiercest form of Lord Shiva. His power lies in putting effort—yatna Shakti—into making gains in life. Hunting, searching, and achieving goals are the basis of yatna shakti. Ardra Nakshatra calls upon one to work hard and persistently to achieve their goals.

The Ardra Nakshatra is good if you need to fight off rivals and enemies, start tasks associated with fire, and for ghost hunting. Considering the fiercely destructible nature of Ardra Nakshatra, it is highly suitable for warfares, to invoke elemental spirits, and for acts of destruction.

Punarvasu - The first three padas of Punarvasu is in Mithuna Rashi, and the last pada is in Karkata Rashi. The ruling of this Nakshatra is Aditi, the Mother Goddess or the devas' mother, and the ruling planet is Guru (Jupiter). The element connected to Punarvasu is water.

People born in this constellation are typically morally and religiously good but can be quite dull and sickly. It would be easy to please people born in this Nakshatra with even small gifts. They are usually a fast walker.

Punarvasu is ruled by the Mother Goddess, known for Her power to gain materialistic wealth and prosperity—referred to as vasutva prapana shakti. She grants abundance to the earth and combines the power of rain or water and air or wind. So, this Nakshatra is great for revitalizing plant life. The power of Punarvasu renews and revitalizes creativity.

Pushya – All the four padas of Pushya Nakshatra are in Karkata Rashi (Cancer). Its ruling planet is Shani, and the ruling lord is Brihaspati, the guru of the devas. It is related to the water element, and the symbol is a cow's teat. Pushya translates to mean nourish, preserve, protect, multiple, strengthen, and replenish. Goddess Lakshmi and Goddess Sita are Pushya Nakshatra natives. People born in Pushya Nakshatra are usually learned, popular, rich, charitable, have control over their passions, adventurous, and lustful. They could be short.

The lord of Pushya Nakshatra is Brihaspati, who is believed to be the god of divine wisdom. He can create spiritual energy— referred to as brahmavarchas shakti. He stands for worshippers and sacrificial worship, both of which are important elements for creating spiritual energy.

He is also the lord of speech, specifically prayer, and all forms of worship, including meditation. Pushya Nakshatra enhances good karma and the outcomes of hard work. This Nakshatra is extremely auspicious to start religious and spiritual practices.

Ashlesha – All the four padas of Ashlesha Nakshatra are in Karkata Rashi. The twin brothers, Lakshman and Shatrughna in Valmiki Ramayana, were natives of this Nakshatra. The ruling planet is Mercury, and the element connected to it is water. The symbol of Ashlesha Nakshatra is a coiled snake.

People born in Aslesha Nakshatra can turn out to be cruel and ungrateful. They pay little attention to the work of other people and can be addicted to various vices. The ruling deity of this Nakshatra is the serpent god who can inflict poison (visasleshana shakti). The serpent god is also connected to trembling and agitation, and these powers can destroy victims.

While this power is good to drop harmful enemies, it can make the natives highly temperamental. Interestingly, serpents are also connected with using practical wisdom, through which one can overcome enemies and other obstacles in their life path.

Magha – All the four padas of Magha Nakshatra are in Simha Rashi (Leo Zodiac). Its ruling planet is Ketu, and its ruling deity is "pitrugan." The symbol of Magha Nakshatra is a royal court with a throne. It is associated with the water element.

People born in Magha Nakshatra are usually wealthy and have many servants to do their bidding. They respect elders and gods and are also very enterprising. Ruled by the "pitrugan" or ancestors, this Nakshatra reflects the power of leaving or giving up one's body—referred to as tyage kshepani shakti. It also represents mourning. Both these characteristic features stand for death or the end of a particular cycle.

Magha Nakshatra is like Bharani Nakshatra, as the latter also represents the soul's movement away from one's body. Another meaning of Magha Nakshatra is related to ancestors and one's pride in ancestral legacy.

This constellation has a cruel and fierce nature and is suitable to undertake tasks related to conflict, deceit, destroying one's enemies, battling and fighting, and other unkind acts. Magha Nakshatra is unsuitable for the start of auspicious activities.

Purva Phalguni – All the four padas of Purva Phalguni Nakshatra are in Simha Rashi. Its ruling planet is Venus, and the ruling deity is Lord Shiva in his Shivalinga form. The symbol of Purva Phalguni is a swinging hammock and is connected with the water element. Goddess Kamakshi or Sri Lalita Tripura Sundari are born in this Nakshatra. It is also the birth star of Guru or Jupiter.

People born in Purva Phalguni Nakshatra are usually fond of traveling—they are wanderers—talk well, loyal, and are good-looking. According to Taittiriya Brahmanas, Purva Phalguni is ruled by Aryaman, the God of unions and contracts, who has the power of procreation—referred to as prajanana shakti. The other qualities of this Nakshatra are those connected with female and male partners.

These powers of Purva Phalguni stand for the union and procreations at all levels of human life, but as Aryaman is the ruler of productive alliances, Purva Phalguni union and procreating powers have approved social and familial agreements.

Uttara Phalguni – The first pada of Uttara Phalguni is in Simha Rashi, and the remaining three padas are in Kanya Rashi. The ruling planet is Surya, and the ruling deity is Aryaman—although Taittiriya Brahmana says that the ruling deity of Uttara Phalguni is Bhaga, the god of happiness. The symbol of this constellation is a bed, and it is associated with the fire element.

People born in Uttara Phalguni are usually happy, popular, and make their own wealth and property. They have the power to subdue their enemies and enjoy all the pleasures of life, including being versed in the arts, association with women, and more.

Bhaga, the god of happiness, is related to the power of accumulating prosperity—referred to as chayani shakti—through unions and marriages. Bhaga's power deals with wealth accumulated from one's own family and wealth derived from the partner's family. So, Uttara Phalguni represents prosperity through unions and marriages.

Hasta – All the four padas are in Kanya Rashi (Virgo Zodiac). Its ruling deity is Surya, and its symbol is a closed hand. It is associated with the fire element. People born in Hasta Nakshatra are usually intelligent, enterprising, enthusiastic, and will serve others, but they can also be thieves, drunkards, and cruel.

According to Taittiriya Brahmana, Hasta Nakshatra is ruled by Savitar, the creative aspect of Surya, the Sun God, who has the power to help one gain what they seek and place it in their hands—referred to as hasta sthapaniya agama shakti. The pursuit of Hasta Nakshatra natives is to seek gains and work toward making the gains. Hasta Nakshatra facilitates the successful and immediate achievement of goals.

Hasta is a swift or light constellation and is good for enjoying luxury items, sports activities and exercises, starting art industries, medical treatments, seeing friends, and fine arts. It is also good for receiving and giving loans.

Chitra – The first two padas of Chitra Nakshatra are in Kanya Rashi, and the last two padas are in Tula Rashi. The ruling planet is Mars or Mangala, and the ruling deity is Vishwakarma, the architect of the gods. Its symbol is the gem found on the serpent's crest.

People born in Chitra Nakshatra love clothes, flowers, and garlands. They are good-looking and kindhearted. They are learned, wealthy, enjoy the pleasures of life, and can be scholarly.

Vishwakarma is known as the cosmic craftsman. The power of Chitra Nakshatra is its ability to accumulate good deeds—referred to as punya chayani shakti. It is also connected with law and truth. These three qualities help people born in Chitra Nakshatra to gain honor in their work or profession.

Chitra Nakshatra allows one to gain the fruit of righteous good deeds. This constellation has a powerful spiritual effect. It is a gentle and soft-natured Nakshatra and is good for making friends, learning fine arts, decorations, and starting auspicious events.

Swati – All the four padas of Swati Nakshatra are in Tula Rashi. The ruling planet is Rahu, its ruling deity is Vayu, the wind god, and its symbol is the buffalo. People born in Swati Nakshatra are usually quiet and mild-mannered. They are skilled in their trade and have great control over their passions.

They are expert orators and can rise to become famous in their area of expertise. They are highly self-restrained and educated. The ruling deity of Swati Nakshatra is Vayu, the God of Wind, who has the power to scatter things (pradhvamsa shakti). Swati Nakshatra is connected with changing forms and moving in various directions. So, this constellation represents transformation.

Vishakha - The first three padas are in the Kanya Rashi, and the fourth pada is in the Vrischika Rashi (Scorpio Zodiac). The ruling planet of Vishakha Nakshatra is Jupiter or Guru, and its ruling deity is Satragni—also known as Indragni. Its symbol is a triumphal gate decked with green leaves.

Vishakha Nakshatra is also called Radha, as it is believed to be complementary to Anuradha Nakshatra. Lord Subramanya or Lord Muruga is born in the Vishakha Nakshatra. Other important people born in this Nakshatra are Lord Buddha, Napoleon, and the Sun God, Surya.

People born in the Vishakha Nakshatra are typically good speakers, good-looking, make a lot of money but also are greedy and jealous. Natives born in this Nakshatra have the power to win over their senses. They are wealthy and miserly.

Vishakha is ruled by Agni and Indra (Indragni). Both these gods together represent the power of heat and light in the atmosphere resulting in the successful fruition of their labors—this power is referred to as vyapana shakti. The star also represents the power of plowing and harvest, which helps one achieve the fruits of their labor, even if these fruits take time to obtain.

Anuradha - All the four padas of Anuradha Nakshatra are in Vrischika Rashi. Its ruling planet is Shani or Saturn, and its symbol is the same as Vishakha Nakshatra, leaf-decked triumphal gates. People born in Anuradha Nakshatra are usually fond of traveling, and many of them are destined to live in foreign countries.

The ruling deity of Anuradha Nakshatra is Mitra, the divine ally with the power of worship—known as aradhana shakti. Mitra is also linked to the right relationships, compassion, and devotion. This constellation is connected to ascension and descension too. All these elements are meant for gaining honor and abundance. Goddess Lakshmi, the goddess of wealth, is of Anuradha Nakshatra.

People born in Anuradha Nakshatra seek balance in their relationships. They give respect and honor as much as they seek the same elements from their partners and friends.

Jyeshtha – All the four padas of Jyeshtha Nakshatra are in Vrischika Rashi. Its ruling planet is Bhuddh or Mercury, and its ruling deity is Lord Indra. The symbol is an earring or a circular talisman that is believed to represent Vishnu's disc's power. The animal symbol of Jyeshtha Nakshatra is a male hare or male deer. Lord Hayagriva, an incarnation of Lord Vishnu, is a native of Jyeshtha Nakshatra.

People born in this constellation are typically charitable, contented, wealthy, and have the power to endure much grief, but they can also be very irritable, have the power to curse others, and be cruel liars.

The ruling deity of Jyeshtha is Lord Indra, the king of devas or gods, who has the power to gain courage in battle and conquer his enemies—referred to as arohana shakti. Jyeshtha Nakshatra also represents the power to attack and defend. All these representations of power are related to heroism.

While Jyeshtha Nakshatra allows one to reach the pinnacle of personal power, it also calls for a lot of courage and effort to do so. This constellation shows that everyone has to win their karmic battles through the effective use of energies and mental powers, and not necessarily through the strength of arms and weapons.

Moola – All the four padas are in Dhanush Rashi (Sagittarius Zodiac). Its ruling planet is Ketu, and its symbol is a cluster of roots. Its ruling deity is Alakshmi or Niritti. The meaning of Moola Nakshatra is also "reverse" or "opposite."

People born in Moola Nakshatra are usually rich, happy, steady, and have a good life, but they can also be liars and trouble others. Niritti or Alakshmi is the goddess of destruction who has the power to destroy and bring about ruin (called barhana shakti). Moola Nakshatra stands for crushing and breaking things.

Moola Nakshatra reflects the importance of destruction in the continuous process of creation. Niritti also stands for Kali or the negative effects of time, which one has to accept as inevitable and use to their advantage.

Purvashadha – All the four padas of Purvashadha are in Dhanush Rashi. Its ruling planet is Venus or Shukra. Its ruling deity is Lord Varuna, the god of water, and its symbol is a hand fan. People born in Purvashadha usually make steady and firm friendships and will get loving spouses.

The power of Varuna, the ruling planet of Purvashada, is the power of invigoration—referred to as varchograhana shakti. This constellation is also connected with strength and relationships or connections. All of these powers are crucial to gain luster in life.

Purvashadha is all about regeneration and purification, like the purifying properties of water. Purification provides one with enhanced energy to strive for goals.

Uttarashadha – The first pada of Uttarashadha Nakshatra is in Dhanush Rashi, and the remaining three padas are in Makar Rashi (Capricorn Zodiac). The ruling planet is Surya, the Sun. The four planks of a bed are its symbol. Lord Ganesh is a native of Uttarashadha.

People born in this constellation are typically polite, virtuous, righteous, and have an attitude of gratitude. The ruling deity of Uttarashadha is Vishwe Deva (or the universal gods), whose power lies in the ability to grant unchallengeable wins and victories. This constellation represents the power to win and the insight of a winnable goal. So, Uttarashadha Nakshatra stands for unchallengeable victories.

Shravana – All the four padas of Shravana Nakshatra are in Makar Rashi. Its ruling planet is Chandra (Moon), and three footprints form its symbol. Its ruling deity is Lord Hari, a form of Vishnu. Shravana Nakshatra is the birth star of Lord Tirupati, Lord Vishnu, and Vamana, the fourth incarnation of the ten avatars of Lord Vishnu.

People born in Shravana Nakshatra are typically learned, liberal, and rich. They will get illustrious spouses toward whom the natives of Shravana Nakshatra will also be loving and affectionate.

Lord Hari, its ruling deity, is known for the power of connection—referred to as samhanana shakti. He is also related to seeking and paths of seeking. These powers together are important elements in building connections. Shravana can link people by connecting their life paths. Vamana, the fourth incarnation of Lord Vishnu, used three strides to connect the three worlds.

Dhanishta – The first two padas of Dhanishta are in Makar Rashi, and the second two padas are in Kumbha Rashi. Its ruling planet is Mars or Mangala, and its ruling deity is Asthavasu. People born in Dhanishta Nakshatra are usually courageous, rich, liberal, and fond of wealth and music. They could also be addicted to vices.

This constellation is ruled by Ashtavasu or the Vasus, who are known for their abundance. The power of the Vasus is connected to abundance and fame—referred to as khyapayitri shakti. Their power is also linked to birth and prosperity. These three powers help in bringing together the resources of different people to work as a team.

The Vasus are the deities of the earth and give abundant gifts to the earthly plane. They also manifest Agni or the sacred fire.

Shatabhistha - All the four padas of Shatabhistha are in Kumbha Rashi. Its ruling planet is Rahu, the symbol is a circle, and its ruling deity is Varuna, the god of water. People born in Shatabhistha Nakshatra are usually truthful and speak plainly. They are quite adventurous, too, but they could be afflicted by suffering from women in their lives. They own large homes and face the ups and downs of life heroically.

Varuna, the god of water, is the ruling deity of Shatabhistha, and he is known for his healing powers (bheshaja shakti). His power also stands for extension, pervasion, and support, all of which help free the world of calamity.

This constellation stands for the power to counter the suffering of difficult karma through repentance and divine grace. The healing powers of Shatabhistha lead to the revitalization of energy.

Purvabhadra - The first three padas are in Kumbha Rashi, and the last pada is in Meena Rashi. The ruling planet is Guru or Jupiter, its symbol is a double-faced man, and its ruling deity is Ajopada, a form of Lord Rudra or Shiva.

People born in Purvabhadra Nakshatra are usually skillful and heroic, but they are likely to face losses and calamities through women, be sorrowful due to the absence of a loved one, and be impatient.

This constellation is ruled by Ajopada or Aja Ekapad, the one-legged serpent, whose power lies in his ability to fire up an individual to achieve spiritual upliftment—referred to as yajamana udyamana shakti. This power is also related to what is good for the people and what is good for the gods. These three elements of this powerful constellation help support the universe, thereby removing the selfishness in people's lives and enhancing their spiritual power.

Uttarabhadra – All the four padas are in Kumbha Rashi. The ruling planet of Uttarabhadra Nakshatra is Shani or Saturn, its ruling deity is Ahirbudhyana, and its symbol is a serpent-like element.

People born in Uttarabhadra Nakshatra are typically witty speakers, morally good, happy, and tend to have many children and grandchildren. The ruling deity Ahirbhudyana is a serpent living in the atmosphere's depths, and its power lies in bringing rain to the earth.

The power of Ahirbhudyana also represents clouds above and the growth of plants below. These three powers represent stability on Earth. This constellation provides growth and prosperity in ways that help the entire world.

Revati – All the four padas of Revati Nakshatra are in Meena Rashi. The ruling planet is Bhuddh or Mercury, and its ruling deity is Pusan, who is the keeper of cows of the gods. Revati is the birth star of Shani.

People born in Revati Nakshatra are usually wealthy, courageous, clean, and have well-developed organs. They are scholarly and charming. Pusan, the ruling deity of Revati Nakshatra, is the Sun God's nourishing aspect, Surya. Its nourishment is symbolized by milk (kshiradyapani shakti).

The power of Pusan also stands for cows and calves. Milk, cows, and calves stand for world nourishment. So, Revati Nakshatra creates abundance and prosperity through nourishment. Pusan is the lord of cattle and the lord of paths. He stands for leading, protecting, and gathering (or herding) people together.

So, now that you have a general idea of Nakshatras through the detailed descriptions of all 27 of them, along with their significance, their ruling deities and planets, and their relationship with the three Gunas, you can move on to learning about Janma Nakshatras in the next chapter.

SECTION TWO: The Lunar Mansions Trilogy

Chapter 3: Janma Nakshatras: The First Nine Nakshatras

Now it is time to look a little deeper into the concept of padas before learning more about Nakshatras. As you already know, each Nakshatra has four padas. The four padas stand for four elements, namely:

- The first pada is Agni because it is mapped to Agni Navamsa

- The second pada is Prithvi – mapped to Prithvi Navamsa

- The third pada is Vayu

- The fourth pada is Jala

These padas also represent Dharma (Agni), Artha (Prithvi), Kama (Vayu), and Moksha (Jala). The four padas are like the four legs of a cow. Each Nakshatra represents a cow. The bull is represented by the Moon, who visits each Nakshatra from the first to the fourth pada, collectively representing Dharma.

During the Satya Yuga, all four legs of Dharma were strong. During the Dwapara Yuga, three were strong, during the Treta Yuga, two were strong, and now, during the Kali Yuga, only one leg of Dharma is strong. So, during the Kali Yuga, it is not just enough to see the Janma Nakshatra but also the pada in which the native was born because only one pada is strong. The rest of the padas are weak.

Here is an example to explain how padas affect natives born in the same Nakshatra. Suppose a person's Janma Nakshatra is Ashwini, first pada. Now, this pada is the Agni pada, which stands for Dharma. So, for this person, Dharma will have a high focus in their life because the other padas, namely Artha, Kama, and Moksha, will be weak.

Similarly, suppose the native was born in the second pada of Ashwini Nakshatra. Then, Artha will be strong for them, and the other three will be weak. Again, if the native is born in Ashwini Nakshatra, the third pada, the Kama aspect will be strong because the others will be weak. For a person born in the fourth pada, Moksha's focus will be strong, and the other three will be weak. That is why it is important to focus on the pada and the Nakshatra to arrive at an accurate birth chart.

The First Nine Nakshatras – Janma Nakshatras

The 27 Nakshatras are divided into nine sets of three Nakshatras each. Everyone has a Janma Nakshatra or the Birth Star. It is the constellation in which the Moon was passing through at the time of one's birth. Janma Nakshatra is the primary driver of personal perceptions, behaviors, prejudices, and instincts and significantly impacts lives.

Janma Nakshatra governs the realities and experiences of life and the way one's mind works. Every constellation has a unique personality composed of likes, dislikes, skill sets, and more. Each Nakshatra has its strengths and weaknesses. None are perfect.

Every Janma Nakshatra has two corresponding constellations linked to it, referred to as Anujanma Nakshatra and Trijanma Nakshatra. For example, if you are born in the first Nakshatra, namely Ashwini, this becomes your Janma Nakshatra. Your Anujanma Nakshatra will be the tenth constellation from Ashwini, namely Makam, and your Trijanma Nakshatra will be the nineteenth constellation, Moolam.

In the same way, each of the 27 Nakshatras has Anujanma and Trijanma Nakshatras linked to it. Here is a list of the first nine constellations. The first column is the Janma Nakshatra, the second column is the Anujanma Nakshatra, and the third column is the Trijanma Nakshatra.

Ashwini – Makam – Moolam

Bharani – Purva Phalguni – Purvashada

Krittika – Uttara Phalguni – Uttarashada

Rohini – Hastha – Shravana

Mrigashirsha – Chitra – Dhanishta

Ardra – Swathi – Satabhishtha

Punarvasu – Vishakha – Purva Bhadrapada

Pushya – Anuradha – Uttara Bhadrapada

Ashlesha – Jyeshtha – Revati

So, the first nine Nakshatras' Anujanma and Trijanma are listed here. Now, suppose your Janma Nakshatra is in the second column of the second set of nine Nakshatras. Then, your Anujanma and Trijanma Nakshatras will be the ones listed in the third and first columns, respectively.

For example, if your Janma Nakshatra is Hashtha, your Anujanma Nakshatra will be Shravana, and your Trijanma Nakshatra will be Rohini. Similarly, if your Janma Nakshatra is Purvashada, your Anujanma and Trijanma Nakshatras will be Bharani and Purva Phalguni, respectively. This chapter deals with the first Nakshatras or the first planetary group.

Every Nakshatra has a symbol assigned to it by the ancient rishis. Each of the symbols and glyphs refers to a particular aspect of human experience connected to the Nakshatra. Multiple symbols are often associated with each Nakshatra considering they affect many areas of human life and experience.

The animal symbol denoted to Nakshatras has a deep meaning to the asterism's nature and character, including its behavioral pattern. The animal connected with each Nakshatra gives a striking indication of the asterism's personality, behavior, and relationships with other constellations.

The Nakshatras are also divided into male and female energies. The masculine Nakshatras are more dynamic than the feminine Nakshatras, which are more passive.

Ashwini

Ashwini occupies 0 degrees to 13 degrees, 20 seconds in Mesha Rashi. The traditional symbol of Ashwini is the head of a horse. It represents the head and is symbolic of the start of the Zodiac. The glyph representing the symbol of Ashwini Nakshatra also stands for the female reproductive system relating to the beginning and initiation of all things.

The activities or actions suitable to be done in Ashwini Nakshatra are:

- Installing an idol or deity or "avahani"
- Thread ceremony or upanayanam
- Parting of the hair on the head or "simontan"

- Shaving or "cuda karanam"

- Starting education or "vidyarambham"

Ashwini is a godly masculine star and has an auspicious nature. Its animal symbol is a horse. The Ashwini Kumaras—to which this star is related—ride a golden chariot, bringing light, happiness, and healing to people. This star denotes the light of dawn, miracle performances, and transportation of goods. The direction of this asterism is forward.

Under the influence of Ashwini Nakshatra, people tend to be full of energy and are ready for adventure and taking risks. It is difficult for them to remain still as they get restless and impatient. They can behave immaturely and do irresponsible acts. This star controls all forms of transportation.

Bharani

Ranging from 13 degrees, 20 seconds to 26 degrees, 40 seconds in Mesha Rashi, Bharani Nakshatra stands for birth, death, and transformation represented by the yoni symbol encapsulated in a triangle. Yoni represents the female vagina, womb, or abode and stands for the feminine reproductive power. The triangle represents the three stars collectively known as the "Buckle of Isis" that make up this constellation or asterism. Ancient astrologers perceived this star as a portal between worlds.

Bharani, a feminine asterism, is good for doing the following activities:

- Nefarious and violent acts

- Entering a tunnel or cave

- Reconcilement activities

- Indulging in swindling and murdering people

- Distilling poison and poisonous medicines

- Activities related to weapons and fire

The direction of this asterism is downward-looking. It has a dreadful nature, and its symbol of a womb represents its ability to hide or eclipse things. The ideas associated with Bharani Nakshatra are suffering and struggle. Ruled by the Lord of Death, Yama, a native of this Nakshatra are usually entangled in the materialistic world. Its animal symbol is an elephant. It is considered the "star of restraint."

Under the influence of Bharani, people tend to struggle through the process of personal growth and transformation. They tend to have self-doubt and be jealous of others, but they are honest and disciplined natives and generally tend to give much importance to their opinions and ideas.

Krittika

Ranging from 26 degrees, 40 seconds in Mesha Rashi to 10 degrees in Vrishabha Rashi, Krittika Nakshatra is represented by a blade or flame metaphorically meaning the "one who cuts." The symbol of Krittika Nakshatra represents its proactive, fiery, and sharp nature.

Krittika's nature is violent, and its direction is downward-looking. This female constellation has a soft/harsh mix of temperament. Krittika means "ax" and represents the physical and creative forces needed to achieve great accomplishments. Ruled by the god of fire, Agni, Krittika asterism brings a burning sensation to the body and mind. This asterism, which has a sheep for its animal symbol, is suitable for the following activities/actions:

- Nefarious and violent activities
- Separation-related and reconciliations activities
- Battles

Considered to be the "star of fire," under the influence of Krittika, people are usually ambitious, passionate, and work determinedly toward their goals. They make great protectors and tend to take very good care of the people they love and are close to.

Rohini

Ranging from 10 degrees to 23 degrees, 20 seconds in Vrishabha Rashi, Rohini is the most materialistic constellation in the Zodiac. Its symbol is the chariot or ox-cart, and the glyph representing Rohini Nakshatra is a four-petaled flower. This glyph is connected to the number four and a rose, the typical emblem of Rohini. Rohini Nakshatra represents the Taurean features of stability, abundance, and fertility. Rohini's animal symbol is a serpent.

Rohini is a female Nakshatra and is suitable for the following activities:

- Installation of a deity/idol
- Thread ceremonies
- House constructions
- Marriages
- Coronations
- Activities of a permanent nature

It has a fixed nature, and natives born in Rohini are likely to be strong and responsible. Its direction is upward-looking and is ruled by Lord Brahma, the creator and the universe's engineer. Rohini is considered to be the "star of ascent." People under Rohini's influence are charming, beautiful, creative, talented, and follow a high standard of living. They are also generally critical of people and look down on others.

Mrigashirsha

Mrigashirsha Nakshatra ranges from 23 degrees, 20 seconds in Vrishabha Rashi up to 6 degrees, 40 seconds in Mithuna Rashi, the symbol of Mrigashirsha is a deer's head. Its glyph resembles a wine cup with a curved surface. The curved surface stands for the deer motif and the horns of Taurus, the bull. Activities suitable for Mrigashirsha are:

- Installation of idol/deity
- Thread ceremonies, marriages
- Travel
- Working with elephants and camels

Its direction is forward-looking. "Mrga" in the name translates to "deer," which means natives usually have an attractive face. This asterism has a soft nature, and natives are typically gentle and involved with research, the poetic, and artworks. This feminine Nakshatra has a serpent as its animal symbol.

Under the influence of Mrigashirsha, people love to travel, seeking new knowledge, and trying to understand their life. They continuously collect and increase their possessions. They are intelligent and are known to uncover hidden things easily.

Ardra

Ranging from 6 degrees, 20 seconds to 20 degrees in Mithuna Rashi, the symbol of Ardra Nakshatra is a teardrop. The teardrop or raindrop glyph has a diamond within it, representing this constellation's theme of growth and renewal through turbulence and chaos.

Ardra, another female Nakshatra, is good for activities like reconcilements and separations and surgical operations. It has a harsh and detestable nature. Its direction is upward-looking and is ruled by Lord Shiva, the destroyer. The animal symbol of Ardra is a dog.

The teardrop symbol of Ardra can also be taken to mean that this asterism is related to the pain and tears of others either by causing them pain or by feeling or empathizing the pain of others; however, the former is more prevalent among natives. Ardra rules over thieves, murderers, and those who create disorder.

Under the influence of Ardra Nakshatra, people are usually quite destructive, but they grow and develop through destruction and suffering. They are also great at using misfortune and difficult situations to their benefit. They are quite distant emotionally and come across as cold and stern.

Punarvasu

Punarvasu Nakshatra ranges from 20 degrees in Mithuna Rashi up to 3 degrees, 20 seconds in Karkataka Rashi. Its symbol is a quiver representing the holder of magical weapons that return to its original abode after completing their mission. The glyph of Punarvasu represents a circular path that shows an arrow leaving the quiver and returning to it, thereby completing the circle. The theme of Punarvasu is that of "becoming good again." Its glyph represents using, recovering, and recycling.

Punarvasu is a godly star and is good for the following activities:

- Thread ceremonies and marriages
- House constructions
- Changing places like moving into new homes, offices, or cities

Its direction is forward-looking and is ruled by Aditi, the mother of the devas. "Puna" translates to "repeat." Hence, Punarvasu is referred to as the "star of renewal." Natives born under Punarvasu usually change homes or professions or even personalities and do not like to be tied down. The star also stands for purification of self. This male Nakshatra's animal symbol is a cat.

Under the influence of Punarvasu, people are typically adept at overcoming challenging and difficult situations. They are inspirational, kind, and have a positive perspective on life. They are quite popular and have a forgiving nature. Also, they are usually content with their lot.

Pushya

Located between 3 degrees, 20 seconds, and 16 degrees, 40 seconds in Karkata Rashi, the symbol of Pushya is a cow's udder. The glyph of Pushya is a circle held within an open four-petaled flower—standing for the four tits of a cow's udder. The circle can be seen as a coconut, a drop of milk, or a wheel, all of which align with Pushya's theme of kindness, generosity, and nourishment.

Pushya is an auspicious star suitable for multiple auspicious beginnings like entering a new home (gruhapravesam), marriages, installation of a deity or idol, etc. When Pushya Nakshatra falls on a Thursday, it is considered an excellent time for all auspicious activities. It is a gentle asterism ruled over by Brihaspati, the guru of the devas. Its direction is upward-looking.

This asterism is believed to be the best among the 27 stars and stands for productivity and nourishment. Natives born in Pushya Nakshatra usually live a happy, flourishing life and can provide for others. Pushya is a masculine Nakshatra, and its animal symbol is a sheep.

Under the influence of Pushya Nakshatra, people give great importance to religion and their beliefs. They are quite arrogant with disagreeing opinions and tend to think they are always right, but they are kind and helpful toward people in need.

Ashlesha

Ashlesha Nakshatra is located between 16 degrees, 40 seconds to 30 degrees in Karkata Rashi. Its symbol is a serpent, which stands for coiling or embracing. Its glyph is represented by two symmetrically intercoiling lines, like the shape of the double-helix DNA. Ashlesha Nakshatra stands for transformative potential and intuition. Ashlesha Nakshatra is feminine, and its animal symbol is a cat.

The activities associated with Ashlesha are argumentation, gambling, falsehood, trade and commerce, burning, and anger. Its direction is downward-looking, and this asterism has a harsh nature. Ashlesha is a demonic star symbolized by a serpent. Natives born in Ashlesha can be anti-social but choose to live an austere life. Ashlesha can bring about pain but also has the potential for great transcendental aspirations.

Ashlesha is considered the "clinging star." People are usually intelligent and wise under its influence, but they often use their knowledge of dark deeds. They also tend to lie and be cunning. However, in the end, they pay for their misdeeds, and through these pains, they grow and develop. They hate being humiliated or criticized.

Chapter 4: Anujanma Nakshatras: The Second Nakshatra Group

The Second Nakshatra Group includes Magha, Purva Pahlguni, Uttara Phalguni, Hasta, Chitra, Swati, Vishakha, Anuradha, and Jyeshtha.

Magha

Magha Nakshatra ranges from 0 degrees to 13 degrees, 20 seconds in Simha Rashi. Its symbol is a throne, and its glyph is a three-pointed crown representing Leonine traits of kingship, honor, pride, duty, respect, and a high position in any hierarchy. Magha is a feminine asterism, and its animal symbol is a rat. Magha is suitable for the following actions/activities:

- Collection works
- Agriculture
- Marriages
- Dances
- Battles

- Works and activities related to weapons and poisons

Its direction is downward-looking. Magha translates into the "mighty one." People born in this Nakshatra usually occupy high and important positions in society and their workplace. Magha stands for pride and dignity. He or she can carry forward family traditions and has the power to lord over the masses.

Natives born in Magha Nakshatra are typically very rich and live in luxury, surrounded by servants to do their bidding. They are learned and have high respect in society, but they fall prey to their attractions to the opposite sex, and their high self-opinion causes them to take on a deep-rooted hatred toward people.

Under Magha's influence, people usually like wealth and power and are willing to work hard to achieve them. They are driven by a need to be recognized wherever they go. They are very loyal to the people they care for.

Purva Pahlguni

Ranging from 13 degrees, 20 seconds to 26 degrees, 40 seconds in Simha Rashi, Purva Phalguni stands for pleasure, delight, comfort, and indulgence. Its symbol is a hammock, and its glyph is a three-curved hammock with a circle within the central upward-turning curve. This hammock or bed represents luxury and a period of relaxation after achieving worldly accomplishments.

This Nakshatra has feminine energy, and its animal symbol is a rat. Activities associated with Purva Phalguni Nakshatra are:

- Wars and battles
- Nefarious and violent activities
- Meat selling
- Swindling and cheating
- Works related to weapons and poisons

Ruled by Venus, the planet of beauty, natives of Purva Phalguni are usually attractive with an ability to sway and influence people sweetly. While the asterism has a nefarious and harsh nature, it is also a lucky star. Purva Phalguni translates to the "fruit of the tree." So, it has the power to bestow good fortune on people. Moreover, the asterism is ruled by Bhagya, the Demi-god of good luck.

Under the influence of Purva Phalguni, people are usually relaxed and carefree. They love to enjoy themselves. They are great communicators and love a hectic social life. They have long-lasting relationships, but they can be very lazy, even if they are talented and creative.

Uttara Phalguni

Uttara Phalguni ranges from 26 degrees, 40 seconds in Simha Rashi to 10 degrees in Kanya Rashi. Its symbol is a fig tree representing comfort and relaxation but with a sense of wisdom rather than indulgence as in Purva Phalguni. Uttara Phalguni is a female star, and its animal symbol is a bull.

The glyph of Uttara Phalguni looks like the three-curved hammock of Purva Phalguni, but the central curve is pointed upwards, and the circle is on top of it, representing an individual who has risen like the sun—unlike the circle in the previous Nakshatra that is blanketed in luxury. The activities associated with Uttara Phalguni are:

- Thread ceremonies
- Installation of idols and deities
- House constructions
- Marriages and coronations

Uttara Phalguni is often translated as a "fig tree" and stands for abundant good qualities and fruitful life. It is referred to as the "star of patronage" because it is focused on helping others. Under the influence of Uttara Phalguni, people are loving and good-natured. They love making friends and have great relationships—and thrive when they are in relationships. They hate being alone and are insecure when they are lonely.

Hasta

Hasta Nakshatra ranges from 10 degrees to 23 degrees, 20 seconds in Kanya Rashi. Its symbol is the human hand, representing work and activities performed by hands, including art and craft. Sometimes, Hasta's glyph is represented by a potter's wheel in the form of an empty circle and five-finger projections pointed upwards. The direction of Hasta is forward-looking.

Hasta is a female asterism, and its animal symbol is buffalo. This asterism is good for the following activities:

- Thread ceremonies
- Construction of houses
- Deity/idol installation
- Marriages
- Coronations

Hasta's hand symbol is often represented as a clenched fist that translates to purity in thought and the power to control. It is deva or godly asterism and has a pleasant temperament. Hasta natives are skilled with their hands, likable and popular, and can remove ignorance and heal.

They are quite orthodox and conservative in their outlook and are inclined toward artistry and public service. They are eloquent speakers and fond of foreign countries. Under the influence of Hasta Nakshatra, people tend to be intelligent and talented. They learn things quickly. They find it difficult to let go of feelings and things. They like to be in professions where they can help others.

Chitra

Chitra Nakshatra ranges from 23 degrees, 20 seconds in Kanya Rashi to 6 degrees, 40 seconds in Tula Rashi. Its symbol is a jewel and is represented by a jewel star. It represents the mind of an artist who is continuously imagining and creating new designs, forms, illusions, and ideas. This feminine constellation is good for the following activities:

- Thread ceremonies
- House constructions
- Installation of idols and deities
- Entering a new home or gruhapravesam

Chitra translates to "beautiful" or "brilliant." It confers a beautiful picture and the ability to arrange things aesthetically. Vishwakarma, the cosmic architect, rules the soft-natured Chitra. Its animal symbol is a tigress.

Under the influence of Chitra, people are typically beautiful and charming. They express themselves well and are good communicators. With a good imagination, natives of Chitra are usually quite artistic. They are excellent at creating new things. The direction of Chitra is forward-looking.

Swati

Swati ranges from 6 degrees, 40 seconds to 20 degrees in Tula Rashi. Its symbol is a coral, and its glyph—a curved line intersecting with a straight line—represents a young shoot being blown by the wind or struck by a sword. The intersection of the curved and straight lines also stands for the balance of contrasting elements and forces. Swati is located halfway through the Nakshatra cycle and connected to compromises and crossroads. The direction of Swati is downward-looking.

Swati, a godly feminine star, is auspicious for the following activities:

- Thread ceremonies
- Entering a new home or gruhapravesam
- House constructions
- Installation of idols and deities
- Marriages

Swati translates to "sword" or "priest." Natives of Swati can cut themselves off from materialism. They love to travel and are learned. Swati natives are self-motivated and have independence in both thought and action. Ruled by Vayu, the wind god, Swat natives are usually slow and deliberate in their movements. The animal symbol of this asterism is the buffalo.

People under the influence of Swati make great artists and are good communicators. They are always curious, which paves the way for them to become learned and scholarly. While they are intuitive and have sharp instincts, Swati natives can also be egoistic and shallow.

Vishakha

Ranging from 20 degrees in Tula Rashi to 3 degrees, 20 seconds in Vrishchika Rashi, Vishakha's symbol is an arch. Its glyph is represented by a triumphal arch, which translates to "two-branched." The Nakshatra itself relates to the single-minded focus needed to achieve goals and the required painful sacrifices for the same. This feminine star has the animal symbol of a tiger. Vishakha is good for the following activities:

- Singing and dancing
- Writing
- Collecting commercial items
- Mechanical works

The direction of Vishakha is downward-looking. Considered the "star of purpose," Vishakha natives are driven by their goals and ambitions. They work hard to achieve their goals. They enjoy competitions and do not back down easily, but they get jealous of others and angry if things don't work out their way.

Vishakha natives are successful even if they are a bit self-centered. A tree with wide-spreading branches often symbolizes Vishakha. This symbol suggests that people under the influence of Vishakha grow in influence and will not stop until their efforts bear fruit.

Anuradha

Anuradha ranges from 3 degrees, 20 seconds to 16 degrees, 40 seconds in Vrischika Rashi. Its symbol is a lotus, and its glyph is also represented by a stick or staff with two young leaves protruding on either side of it. Anuradha reflects "success achieved subsequent" to the single-minded focus of Vishakha. Anuradha is a male Nakshatra, and its animal symbol is a rabbit. Sometimes, the animal symbol of Anuradha is taken to be a female deer. This asterism is good for the following activities:

- Marriages
- Gruhapravesam
- Thread ceremonies
- Reconcilements and separations
- House construction
- Installation of idols and deities

Its direction is forward-looking and is ruled by Mitra, a demigod associated with the sun god. Anuradha is considered to be the "star of calling others to action" and the "star of success." People born in Anuradha Nakshatra are great at organizing, and hence, make excellent leaders. Radha is the feminine energy that encourages everyone to serve the lord.

Under the influence of Anuradha, people are generally great organizers. They balance their work and relationships very well. They are flexible and can cooperate with others easily, both useful elements in teamwork, which, in turn, make them great leaders. They love to make friends and are good at sharing.

The stick or staff also stands for a magician's wand. Anuradha has the power to convert Vishakha's narrow-minded goal-oriented approach to a wide vision of awe and reverence for the entire universe.

Jyeshtha

Ranging from 16 degrees, 40 seconds to 30 degrees in Vrischika Rashi, Jyeshtha translates to "the eldest" and stands for authority. Its symbol is an amulet, and its glyph is a double-edged circular earring-like amulet with three lines connecting the outer and inner circles. Jyeshtha Nakshatra represents experience, expertise, and seniority. The three lines stand for the past, present, and future.

Jyeshtha is a female asterism, and its animal symbol is the rabbit. Often, its animal symbol is also taken to be a male deer. Jyeshtha is an auspicious star for the following activities:

- Commerce
- Writing
- Mechanical works
- Dancing and music

Jyeshtha Nakshatra has a sharp and forceful nature. Translating to "chief" or "senior-most," Jyeshtha Nakshatra confers natives with the power to achieve executive positions in their professions. Jyeshtha natives invariably get what they want. The star is ruled by Lord Indra, who bestows the power to get things done with goals achieved skillfully.

Under the influence of Jyeshtha Nakshatra, people tend to be great at wielding power and responsibility positions. Wise and intelligent, they are skilled at looking after their families and the people they care for. They are typically leaders of their house and their professional teams, but they tend to face many difficulties and hardships in their lives. They are not very social beings and have only a handful of trusted people around them.

Influence of Anujanma Nakshatras

The Anujanma Nakshatras stands for intervening elements that connect the past karma of a native and their present karma. The Anujanma Nakshatra demonstrates the potency or ability of a native to analyze, execute, and achieve the present's karma as connected with the past. The planets of the Anujamna Nakshatra should not be inimical with the planets of the Janma Nakshatra.

For example, if a native has Saturn in their Lagna or the house of the planet of their birth star, and Mars is in the fourth-star house from their Lagna, the chances of such individuals to make rash and wrong decisions are high. This happens because Mars and Saturn are inimical, with one in the Janma Nakshatra and the other in the Anujanma Nakshatra.

Chapter 5: Trijanma Nakshatras: The Last Nakshatra Group

The last group of Nakshatras forming the Trijanma Nakshatras for the first group include Moola, Purvashada, Uttarashada, Shravana, Dhanishta, Shatabishtha, Purva Bhadrapada, Uttara Bhadrapada, and Revati.

Moola

Located in the Dhanush Rashi (Sagittarius) from 0 degrees to 13 degrees, 20 seconds, Moola Nakshatra stands for "root" or "center" and is often referred to as the "root star." This Nakshatra represents the galactic center. Rightly so, the symbol of Moola is a bundle of roots.

The symbol is represented by three straight lines passing through the circumference and intersecting at the center of a circle. Two of the three straight lines bend and form lines that appear to meet toward each other. This glyph of a bundle of roots stands for Moola's desire to seek and discover the essential nature of all things in the universe. Additionally, roots also represent medicine. Moola, a masculine star, is good for the following activities:

- Acts of violence and nefariousness

- War

- Marriages

- Medication

Its direction is downward-looking, and its animal symbol is a dog. Under the influence of Moola, people seek the core principle of all things in life. The bundle of roots also stands for the natives' feelings of being tied or bound to misfortunes and suffering. Moola's nature is sharp and violent. Natives of Moola Nakshatra are clever, capable, and even spiritually devoted, but they always look at everything around them with a sense of mistrust.

Moola influences people to be good investigators who are skilled at uncovering hidden truths. The various ups and downs they face make them feel a deep sense of loss and pain. They are usually resentful and often blame others for their problems.

Purvashada

Purvashada Nakshatra extends from 13 degrees, 20 seconds to 26 degrees, 40 seconds in Dhanush Rashi. Its symbol is a fan, and its glyph is represented by a figure of eight, with the top circle being larger than the bottom circle. Another circle is embedded in the top curvature of the number eight. This glyph looks like a seashell from which Venus, the ruling planet of this Nakshatra, emerges. It also resembles the symbol of Purvashada, namely a fan.

Referred to as the "invincible star" and represented by a monkey, Purvashada is good for the following activities:

- Work concerning weapons and poisons

- Murder and killing actions

- Swindling and cheating

Its direction is downward-looking, and it has a violent, argumentative nature. Natives are typically humble and have a large family. They are faithful in their relationships and are likely to sit in high positions at their workplace and in society.

Under the influence of Purvashada, people are strong and independent. They continually strive hard to improve their status. With great communication, natives have good manipulation and influencing skills, but they tend to have anger issues and get aggressive.

The fan symbol of Purvashada has multiple connotations. It could be used to stoke the fire to keep the passion alive or to cool off the fire, which means to survive adversity, as a decorative item (standing for art and crafts), or as a symbol of mystery by hiding one's face behind the fan.

Uttarashada

Ranging from 26 degrees, 20 seconds in Dhanush Rashi up to 10 degrees in Makar Rashi (Capricorn), Uttarashada's symbol is a tusk. Its glyph is represented by two elephant tusks crossing over each other on a pyramid, rising from between the tusks. The pyramid represents the crystallization of power, the tusks stand for Lord Ganesha, the remover of obstacles, and the sun is the ruling planet of Uttarashada.

Uttarashada is a masculine star with a mongoose as its animal symbol. Its direction is upward-looking, and it has an auspicious nature. Ruled by the Sun God, Uttarashada reflects leadership qualities. It is referred to as the "universal star," which means natives can relate to others and work toward uplifting people around them. Uttarashada is good for:

- Deity/idol installation
- Marriages and coronations

Under the influence of Uttarashada, people are typically kind, soft-natured, and patient. They have immense enduring power. They are responsible and work hard with a determination to achieve their goals. They are truthful and sincere, but if they lose interest in what they are doing, they become lazy.

Shravana

The meaning of Shravana is "to listen," and its symbol is an ear. This Nakshatra ranges from 10 degrees to 23 degrees, 20 seconds in Makar Rashi, and it stands for not only listening to others but also listening to one's inner voice.

Its glyph is represented by the full moon, its ruling planet, supported underneath by a crescent moon. Three uneven straight lines emerge from the circumference of the full moon. The three straight lines have a small circle at their ends. The small circles represent the "three uneven steps" connected to Shravana. The three lines represent the connection between the speaker and the listener.

Shravana is a masculine star, and its animal symbol is a monkey. Shravana is believed to be the "star of learning" and has a deep connection to Goddess Saraswati and Lord Vishnu in his dwarf form. Shravana stands for understanding and communication of that knowledge, which helps people to transcend the material world.

Under its influence, people are usually wise and intelligent. They always seek knowledge, are good listeners, and make good teachers. They are usually quite restless and want to travel from place to place in search of new knowledge.

Dhanishta

Dhanishta ranges from 23 degrees, 20 seconds in Makar Rashi up to 6 degrees, 40 seconds in Kumbh Rashi (Aquarius). Its symbol is a drum, and its glyph also represents a drum. From the side, the glyph of Dhanishta looks like a standing drum with three intersecting lines. Dhanishta is a bold and confident Nakshatra and stands for music and dance, representing the larger rhythm of life.

The glyph also represents the rhomboid pattern of the placement of the stars in this constellation. The three intersecting lines on the transverse angle of the standing drum form eight unequal triangles. These triangles represent the eight Vasus, the presiding deities of Dhanishta.

Dhanishta is a female constellation with a lion as its animal symbol. It is a good star for the following activities:

- Upanayanam or thread ceremonies
- Gruha pravesam or entering a new home
- Taking medication
- House construction

Its direction is upward-looking, and the planet Mars rules it. The symbol of a drum represents talent or an interest in music and dance. It is referred to as the "star of the symphony," which also stands for the natives' ability to unify people toward a common cause.

Under the influence of Dhanishta, people are wealthy and have many possessions. They are artistic and inclined to music and dance, but like the drum—its symbol—natives tend to be hollow and are continually looking for external things to fill this emptiness, an attitude that makes them highly self-absorbed.

Shatabhisha

Ranging from 6 degrees, 40 seconds to 20 degrees in Kumbha Rashi, Shatabhisha's symbol is 1,000 stars. Shatabhisha stands for a "hundred healers." Its glyph is an empty circle from which four lightning bolts emerge, representing the presence of electricity in everything. Two small circles adorn the top and bottom of the circular glyph. These little circles represent electrons going around the atomic nucleus.

From above, the glyph of Shatabhisha looks like a turtle with its four limbs outstretched. The turtle is seen as a carrier of the world. The glyph stands for the transpersonal nature of this rather reclusive, eccentric, and mystical asterism.

Shatabisha is a female asterism, and its animal symbol is a mare. It is upward-looking and is good for the following activities:

- House construction
- Entering a new home
- Installing deities/idols
- Thread ceremonies
- Taking medicines
- Horse riding

It has a cruel, detestable nature and is ruled by Rahu. Translating to "the hundred physicians," this Nakshatra represents physicians and healers. Referred to as the "veiling star," Shatabhisha reflects quietude and feelings of difficulties concerning self-expression.

Under the influence of Shatabhisha, people are generally philosophical and highly secretive. They can be great healers, but they are moody and lonely, considering they lack good communication skills. They also tend to have an unreasonably high opinion about themselves and believe they know everything, which comes across as arrogance.

Purva Bhadrapada

Purva Bhadrapada ranges from 20 degrees in Kumbha Rashi up to 3 degrees, 20 seconds in Meena Rashi (Pisces). Its symbol is a funeral cot or bed. Its glyph represents two faces of a man standing for the moment of death, during which one exists both in this world and in the next.

The glyph of a Purva Bhadrapada is a circle with a horizontal chord on the upper hemisphere, a vertical diagonal intersecting this chord, and two small, uneven horizontal lines intersecting the diagonal in the lower hemisphere. A sword also represents Purva Bhadrapada, and the diagonal of the circle represents the sword, which stands for severance.

Purva Bhadrapada is a masculine star with a lion as its animal symbol. It is a star for the following activities:

- Argument-related works
- Nefarious and violent tasks
- Meat selling
- Battles and wars
- Killing

It has a dreadful nature. The star translates to "the burning pair"—along with the next star, namely Uttara Bhadrapada—and represents an impetuous and passionate individual who usually has an unstable mind, but because Jupiter rules it, they tend to have a repentant nature and accept and learn from their mistakes. It is also referred to as the "star of transformation."

Under its influence, people are indulgent and passionate in all their works. They are quite secretive and two-faced. They are good communicators and can influence people.

Uttara Bhadrapada

Uttara Bhadrapada ranges from 3 degrees, 20 seconds to 16 degrees, 40 seconds in Meena Rashi. Its symbol is a water snake, and its glyph represents this. It is a serpentine, snake-like line slithering around and upward on a vertical axis, stick, or staff. The deity of this constellation is Ahirbudhanya, or the "Serpents of Death" represented in the glyph.

Like Purva Bhadrapada, Uttara Bhadrapada also connects to death, though in a different form. This asterism represents consciousness sinking deep into an abyss or the super consciousness. Uttara Bhadrapada stands for the deep levels of unconsciousness and the prana or life force within it.

This male asterism has a cow for its animal symbol and, together with Purva Bhadrapada, is referred to as the "burning pair." This star reflects the power to control anger and move from lower materialistic consciousness to higher spiritual consciousness.

Under its influence, people are generally good at controlling their emotions. They tend to be lazy but are cheerful and kind. They are highly protective of the people they love and care for. They love home and family and all the simple good things that come with their loved ones.

Revati

Revati Nakshatra ranges from 16 degrees, 40 seconds to 30 degrees in Meena Rashi. Its symbol is a fish, and its glyph is two intersecting circular sectors (fish-like) with an eye in the center. Revati also means "to transcend" and "wealth." Revati absorbs and synthesizes the mysteries of the previous 26 asterisms, an element represented by the all-seeing eye between the intersecting fish-like structures.

Revati is a female asterism and has an elephant for its animal symbol, which reflects material prosperity. Revati is related to the following activities:

- Thread ceremony
- Installation of idols/deities
- Recovering and overcoming drug addiction
- Gruha pravesam

Revati translates to "wealth" and is ruled by Pusha, a deva known for his shepherding and protecting nature. Under the influence of Revati, people are generally helpful, loving, and kind. They are positive people and have a happy disposition. They enjoy making new friends and love being social. They are caregivers too. Being the last Nakshatra, Revati indicates the final journey, from this world to the next.

Different Types of Karma

Karma is a supremely important element in Hinduism. A simple definition of karma is that it represents the fruits of one's past and present actions, which, in turn, impact the fruits of the future. The literal translation of "karma" is action in Sanskrit. There are typically three types of karma:

- Sanchita Karma
- Prarabdha Karma
- Aagami Karma

Sanchita Karma – This baggage of karma is accumulated past actions waiting to come to fruition. Sanchita is like a storehouse that holds all the actions of your past lifetimes. It is a collection of unresolved karmas waiting to achieve resolution status.

Prarabdha Karma – This karma is what you are doing now, in this lifetime, and the fruits of your present actions.

Agami Karma – Future actions resulting from your current karma are collectively referred to as Agami Karma. Resolving and mitigating past karma create new karmas that may or may not be resolved in this lifetime. The results of the current karmas carried into the future are referred to as Agami Karma.

The Janma Nakshatra, Anujanma Nakshatra, and the Trijanma Nakshatra are rooted in your past and present karmas. Of all the planets, Rahu and Ketu are considered the most closely associated with karmas and their fruitions. The ancient Vedic seers categorized these two shadow planets as the most mysterious heavenly bodies that profoundly affect people's lives, depending on their karmas, based on which they posit themselves on their birth chart.

Every one of the seven planets with a physical presence affects and influences your present life on Earth. On the other hand, Rahu and Ketu are believed to be "invisible" energy forms that can access karmas from past lives, namely the Sanchita Karmas.

Ketu is considered the oldest planet as he existed even at the time of cataclysms of nature. Therefore, all your past lives' karmas are recorded in Ketu's registry. His records indicate the area in which you have been working during previous lifetimes. Rahu, being the second oldest planet according to Vedic Astrology, holds the information regarding your future.

Therefore, Ketu gives an indication of talents, which you have been polishing up on in previous incarnations and come naturally in the present life. In summary, Ketu stores your past, and Rahu stores your future.

Effects of Planets in Various Houses

Here are some examples of how planets affect natives as they pass through the various houses of the Zodiac.

When Saturn is in the ninth house, he brings about losses in finance. Natives are likely to face obstacles when performing good actions. Close relatives could die, and there could be perpetual sorrow. In the tenth house, Saturn drives the natives to do some sinful action. Also, there could be a loss of honor for natives. They could suffer from diseases.

Saturn in the eleventh house brings happiness and wealth to the natives. They are likely to receive great honors too. Saturn in the twelfth house is likely to drive the natives to pursue worthless and fruitless businesses. Natives are likely to be robbed of their wealth, and spouses and children could fall sick.

Rahu in the Janma Rashi or the first house brings about death or sickness. In the second, fifth, seventh, and ninth houses, natives lose wealth, money, etc. In the third, sixth, and eleventh houses, Rahu brings happiness. In the fourth, he brings sorrow. Rahu in the eighth house brings danger to the life of the native. In the tenth house, Rahu brings about gain for the natives. In the twelfth house, Rahu brings about expenditure.

Sun and Mars affect the natives only during the first 10 degrees of a house, whereas Venus and Jupiter affect when they are in the center of the house, and the powers of Saturn and Moon are effective when they are in the last part—last 10 degrees of the Zodiac—through which they are passing. The effect of Rahu and Mercury are felt right across the 30 degrees of any given Zodiac.

SECTION THREE: Lunar Mansions in Predictive Astrology

Chapter 6: Timing of Events: Udu-Dashas

Predictive Astrology or Phalita Jyotishya—which translates to "that which will fructify"—deals with karma, actions, and behaviors that define one's destiny. This sub-branch of astrology also deals with how you can reverse earlier mistakes and wrongdoings through penance, worship, charity, etc.

Your horoscope is like a snapshot of the heavens, as seen from your place and time of birth. However, the planets are not fixed or frozen. They are continuously moving. Hindu Astrology, therefore, has two types of movements of Grahas or planets. One type is called transits or direct movement of planets in its ecliptic. Another type of movement is referred to as progressed or projected movement, which, in Vedic Astrology, is termed as Dashas.

Timing of Events is a unique feature of Vedic Astrology. Vimshottari Dasha is an essential tool and technique used in Jyotishya to time events. This highly popular system has been in use for centuries and is employed both by amateurs, in its basic forms, and professional astrologers, in its advanced and basic forms.

Vimshottari Dasha is based on the Moon or Chandra's position on a Nakshatra, and therefore, is a Nakshatra Dasha. The first Nakshatra—as you already know—is Ashwini, which is ruled by Ketu. The second Nakshatra is Bharani, ruled by Venus or Shukra. This list continues until the 27th Nakshatra, Revati, ruled by Mercury or Bhuddh. Another popular Dasha is called Kalachakra, and it incorporates both Rashis and Nakshatras.

Understanding Udu Dasha

Udu translates to "flying," a term also used for Nakshatras. Ideally, all Nakshatra Dashas are Udu Dasha. However, in practice, Vimshottari Dasha is considered to the "The Udu Dasha." Astrologers have used this Dasha as the primary staple for centuries. However, in recent times, astrologers like B V Raman, Sri Sanjay Rath, and Sri K. N. Rao have studied and produced a large body of work dealing with multiple other Dashas.

The primary and most basic premise behind the concept of Dashas is this: Life is sectioned into different segments or periods represented by planets (Nakshatra Dasha) or signs (Rashi Dasha) in the horoscopes. The orientation point for Nakshatra Dasha is the natal moon. Now, visualize the moon's progress from the moment of a native's birth through the rest of the Zodiac at a slower speed than its direct movement speed, which is about two and a half days per sign.

As the Moon or Chandra passes through the different Nakshatras, the planet lordship also changes. The planetary lord or ruler is considered to be the main planet indicator during the period Chandra passes through that Nakshatra. Some Dashas, including the most popularly used, namely Vimshottari Dashas, have a very long total duration. For example, in the Vimshottari Dasha, the natal moon takes 120 years to transit through the entire Zodiac, and therefore, most individuals do not complete the entire cycle in their lifetime.

Vimshottari Dasha System and Nakshatras

According to the Vimshottari Dasha system, each of the nine planets in Vedic Astrology rule over varying periods, the total of which is 120 years.

- Ketu rulers for seven years

- Venus rules for twenty years

- The Sun rules for six years

- The Moon rules for ten years

- Mars rules for seven years

- Rahu rules for eighteen years

- Jupiter rules for sixteen years

- Saturn rules for nineteen years

- Mercury rules for seventeen years

Although there is no rationale behind the formation of the Vimshottari Dasha System and the ruling periods, some experts have grouped the periods into two categories by an imaginary line between the Moon and the orienting (or Udu) point in the Vimshottari scheme and have come up with the following:

- The periods of Saturn, Jupiter, Rahu, and Mars total 60 years – this is one category.

- The periods of the Moon, the Sun, Venus, Ketu, and Mercury total 60 years – this is the second category.

Therefore, the outer planets are placed in the first group while the two luminaries, namely the Sun and Moon, along with the inner planets, are placed in the second group. In the Udu Dasha system, the natal moon's sidereal constellation position is taken as the point at which the native enters the 120-year cycle. In the 360-degree ecliptic, there are 27 constellations measuring 13 degrees, 20 minutes each. It starts at Aries (0-degrees), which is ruled by Ketu.

Ketu is followed by Venus, Surya (Sun), Chandra (Moon), Mangala (Mars), Rahu, Jupiter (Guru), Shani (Saturn), and Mercury (Bhuddh) in the same order. This order repeats until all the 27 asterisms are covered. Each Vimshottari Dasha period (called mahadasha) is further subdivided into nine sub-periods called antardashas or bhuktis.

The first bhukti or antardasha is ruled by the lord of the mahadasha and is followed by the bhuktis of the remaining eight in the same order. For example, in the Sun's Mahadasha, the first antardasha will be ruled by Sun himself, followed by the Moon, Mars, Rahu, Jupiter, Saturn, Mercury, Venus, and Ketu.

Each of the antardashas can be further divided into antaras, pratyantaras, sukshmas, and more. However, going into these finer divisions' practical usefulness is far less than the cumbersomeness and uncertainty behind the accuracy of such data. Therefore, most astrologers do not go deeper than the antardasha period.

The Vimshottari Dasha System follows the power of the Lords who rule over the Nakshatras. Here is a list of the 27 Nakshatras and the planet lords that rule them for better understanding. This list is given planet-wise:

1. Ketu rules over Ashwini, Magha, and the Moola (the first, tenth, and nineteenth Nakshatras)

2. Venus or Shukra rules over Bharani, Purva Phalguni, and Purvashadam (the second, eleventh, and twentieth Nakshatras)

3. Sun or Surya rules over Krittika, Uttara Phalguni, and Uttarashada (the third, twelfth, and 21st Nakshatras)

4. Moon or Chandra rules over Rohini, Hasta, and Shravana (the fourth, thirteenth, and 22nd Nakshatras)

5. Mars or Mangala is the lord of Mrigashirsa, Chitra, and Dhanista (the fifth, fourteenth, and 23rd Nakshatras)

6. Rahu is the lord of Ardra, Swati, and Shatabhishta (the sixth, fifteenth, and 24th Nakshatras)

7. Jupiter or Guru is the lord of Punarvasu, Vishakha, and Purva Bhadrapada (the seventh, sixteenth, and 25th Nakshatras)

8. Saturn of Shani is the lord of Pushya, Anuradha, and Uttara Bhadrapada (the eighth, seventeenth, and 26th Nakshatras)

9. Mercury or Bhuddh is the lord of Ashlesha, Jyestha, and Revati (the ninth, eighteenth, and 27th Nakshatras)

Therefore, Ketu, Venus, the Sun, the Moon, Mars, Rahu, Jupiter, Saturn, and Mercury—in that order—rule over three Nakshatras each. The three Nakshatras in one set, ruled by one planet lord, form the Janma, Anujanma, and Trijanma Nakshatras for each other. Further, every planet has a sign of exaltation Zodiac sign, which is as follows:

• The Sun's exaltation sign is Aries or Mesha Rashi

• The Moon's exaltation sign is Taurus or Vrishabha Rashi

• Rahu's exaltation sign is Gemini or Mithuna Rashi

• Jupiter's exaltation sign is Cancer or Karkata Rashi

• Mercury's exaltation sign is Virgo or Kanya Rashi

• Saturn's exaltation sign is Libra or Tula Rashi

• Ketu's exaltation sign is Sagittarius or Dhanush Rashi

• Mars's exaltation sign is Capricorn or Makar Rashi

• Shukra's exaltation sign is Pisces or Kumbha Rashi

Nakshatras and Planet Transits

The Navatara and Tara Bala system is a Nakshatra predictive system used to understand the planets' transits through the various Rashis. This system tracks the transits of important and key Nakshatras from the Lagna or the birth Nakshatra. For example, if your birth Nakshatra is Jyeshtha, this becomes your Janma Nakshatra, and the counting for the Navatara and Tara Bala system starts from Jyeshtha. Then, the first nine Nakshatras for you would be as follows:

1. Jyeshtha

2. Moola

3. Purvashada

4. Uttarashada

5. Shravana

6. Dhanishta

7. Shatabisha

8. Purva Bhadrapada

9. Uttara Bhadrapada

These first nine Nakshatra counted from your Janma Nakshatra hold far more potency to deliver effects than the second and third tier of nine Nakshatras. This concept, referred to as Udu-Dashas, has a deep connection to Dasas and planet transits.

Further, according to Andrew Foss, a Vedic Astrologer of high repute and author of the best-selling book *Yoga of the Planets*, these nine important aspects of your life are connected to planetary rulers and the sequence of the Dasha system. Read on to find out how the Dashas affect these nine important aspects of your life.

Janma or Your Birth – This crucial aspect of your life is related to the first house in the Udu-Dasha system. Mercury and Ketu influence this aspect. Your Janma is connected to your birth Nakshatra which, according to the Udu-Dasha system, becomes the first Nakshatra for you, and the tenth and the nineteenth asterisms, which are your Anujamna and Trijanma Nakshatras.

Your birth star governs everything in your life. Furthermore, the moon is connected to your mind, and the star under the moon's influence becomes the seat of your soul. The birth star and your first house represent a focused form of your ability to synthesize all your life experiences using your intelligence.

The ruler of this aspect, Mercury, also governs early childhood, and this planet's influence and position determine the status of your birth, the development of your thought process, and education during that time of your life.

Andrew Foss says this about the Janma Nakshatra: "It is the fruit empowered to fulfill our desires depending on what we deserve." Now, when Saturn transits through your birth star, it shakes up certain things in your life because Saturn is a natural enemy of Mercury and Ketu. Therefore, your health could be challenged, which can be seen as a reminder to seek liberation (or moksha) in this lifetime.

The birth star for most astrologers is a point of conflict. Some believe that the first house is beneficial, and some think it is malefic. Therefore, it makes sense to accept a balanced approach to this crucial house. The birth star mostly supports the native, yet the beneficial effects could fall prey to hidden challenges or connection to the eighth house.

Janma Nakshatras, which are one, ten, and nineteen, are connected to Mercury. If your birth Nakshatra is also ruled by Mercury, all the other asterisms owned by Mercury will have a Janma relationship in your horoscope.

Sampat - Sampat is related to gains. The status of your second and eleventh house—counted from Lagna—determines this factor in your life and is ruled by Venus. The Sampat houses are the second, eleventh, and twentieth Nakshatras from your Janma Nakshatra and are ruled by Venus. Number 2 in Vedic Astrology is always related to the accumulation of wealth, gains, and profits.

Therefore, in your Rashi Chart or birth chart, benefic planets placed here during their Dasas bring gains for you, and malefic planets could bring losses and a sense of deprivation. Transits through the second star are gainful for the native. Therefore, Jupiter transiting through the second star can be particularly profitable for the naïve as this planet is connected to good fortune, acquisitions, blessings, and prosperity.

To illustrate with an example, if your birth star is Swait, Jupiter will bring gains and profits when it is transiting through Vishakha. Similarly, for a native born in Jyestha Nakshatra, Moola would be the second Nakshatra, which means all Ketu stars will bring good fortune for this native whenever benefic planets transit through them.

Vipat - Another critical life element, Vipat, is all about dangers to your wealth and money. This aspect is connected to the eighth and twelfth houses, counted from your Lagna, and is ruled by Sun, the planet connected to wealth. Vipat Nakshatra is the third asterism from your natal moon. The third Nakshatra has the power to destroy adharma and people who do not follow dharma.

As it is ruled by the Sun, the planet related to wealth, the third Nakshatra position is important for obtaining or losing wealth. You already know that Sun and Saturn are bitter enemies. Therefore, it is easy to understand that you are likely to face significant financial problems when Saturn transits through the third house.

For example, if your Janma Nakshatra is Jyeshta, the third Nakshatra would be Purvashada. When Saturn transits through this Nakshatra, its energy to create financial problems for the concerned native will be triggered. Vimpat positions can lead to the native making bad decisions and putting forth multiple challenges for them during major transits like Saturn, Rahu, or Ketu. It is also connected to the twelfth house, which is also related to the loss of wealth. A positive way of looking at such seeming losses is that these difficult times drive one to look spiritually upwards and find their path to liberation.

Kshema – Kshema relates to happiness and security in your life, is connected to the fourth Nakshatra, and is ruled by Moon. The fourth, thirteenth, and 22nd Nakshatras from your birth star are related to Kshema, which is associated with a disease-free life of comfort and ease. The fourth Nakshatra is connected with the feelings of security that the native gets.

Therefore, when benefic planets like Jupiter and Venus transit through the fourth, thirteenth, and 22nd Nakshatras, the native may have a substantial improvement in their state of happiness. On the other hand, malefic planets like Ketu could result in unhappy disruptions to the native's life.

Prayatak – Prayatak is related to obstacles and enemies, is ruled by Mars, and is managed by the fifth, fourteenth, and 23rd Nakshatras from your Janma Nakshatra. This aspect of your life is connected to the third and sixth houses. It is related to enemies and rivals who can instill fear of destruction in the native.

Mars, the ruler of this position and aspect, is the lord who prevents you from violating your dharma. After all, no one really wants to do wrongful deeds to face the wrath of a weapon-wielding warrior like Mars. So, fear helps keep your adharma actions in check.

With Mars ruling this life aspect, there is bound to be frustrations and indecisions when Saturn, the enemy of Mars, transits through this Nakshatra. The primary objective of the fifth Nakshatra is to fight and compete to do your dharma. Therefore, if your birth Nakshatra is Vishakha when Saturn transits through Purvashada, you are likely to face the malefic effects of Saturn even if your Sade Sati is three signs away.

Sadhana – Sadhana is the fulfillment, accomplishments, and attainment of desires and is ruled by Rahu. The life element is connected to the eleventh house. Sadhana is managed by the sixth, fifteenth, and 24th Nakshatras from your birth asterism. Benefic planets transiting through the sixth Nakshatra will bring fruits, while malefic planets will bring forth struggle and prevent opportunities from being available.

Interestingly, because Rahu is connected to this Nakshatra, desires and accomplishments may be fulfilled through unethical and devious means. For example, if your birth star is Chitra, when Saturn transits through Purvashada—the sixth Nakshatra from your Janma Nakshatra—this period could get support through the transits, and your desires could lead to fruition, provided it all fits in with the context of your Dasha period.

Naidhana or Vadha – This interesting and important part of your life deals with changes driven by the death or destruction of old things and elements. It is ruled by Jupiter and is connected to the eighth house. It is represented by the seventh, sixteenth, and 23rd Nakshatras from your birth star.

When malefic planets like Rahu, Ketu, or Saturn transit through the seventh, sixteenth, and 23rd Nakshatras, the native is likely to face challenges. These life experiences are also connected to the eighth house from the Lagna, where malefic planets can bring about acute illnesses, sudden accidents, or divorces without warning. The eighth house experiences are excellent lessons for one to transcend beyond the mundane materialism and search for the true meaning and purpose of life.

Mitra - Life without partners and friends is not worth living. Your horoscope helps you determine how your friends and partners will help or harm you by studying the "mitra" aspect of your life, which Saturn rules and is related to the seventh house and the eighth, seventeenth, and 26th Nakshatras from your birth star.

Saturn appears to be an unusual ruler in this place, considering this aspect deals with friends and progress. Andrew Foss explains that the fulfillment of desire after waiting so long—in that you have forgotten you had the desire at all—is a reflection of Saturn's power to do good by making you work hard, responsibly, and with patience. His seemingly malign attitude shows that your laziness and irresponsible behavior will not bring your desires to fruition.

Param Mitra - This aspect deals with great friends and spiritual fulfillment. Ruled by Ketu, it is related to the ninth and twelfth houses from your Lagna and the ninth, eighteenth, and 27th Nakshatras from your Janma Nakshatra. In the ninth Nakshatra and ninth house, all planets support the native and bring good fortune.

The ninth Nakshatra is connected to Ketu, a planet reflecting the time and place where your karma's and desires' ultimate liberation and fruition are completed. The ninth house is the peak of your accomplishments. Benefic planets transiting through the ninth Nakshatra are bound to hold great promise for natives.

Importantly, Dasha's effects should be read or studied by themselves. You must refer to the birth chart and the transits. The stars of the dashas and the asterisms' and planet lords' dispositions represent sensitive areas in the concerned native's life. Therefore, all aspects of astrology have to be taken into account to arrive at accurate and sensible predictions.

Chapter 7: Nakshatras and Relationship Compatibility

Relationship and marriage compatibility is not just an interesting topic but an essential element in Predictive Vedic Astrology. In Indian culture, where arranged marriages are the norm, comparing horoscopes to see if the potential couple are suitable for each other is the starting point of any marriage plans. Moreover, multiple cases have proved the efficacy of horoscope comparisons before arranging marriages. The interest and the intrigue behind the concept are, of course, unmistakable. Therefore, this chapter is part of this book on Nakshatras.

Just to give you an overview at this juncture, there are 27 Nakshatras in the Zodiac, each having four padas or quarters. The asterisms are connected to different Rashis or Zodiac Signs, as well as the nine planets. The star in which you were born is referred to as the birth star. If you start counting from here, your birth star is #1. The tenth star from here counted in Nakshatras' accepted order—from Ashwini to Revati—will be your Anujanma Nakshatra, and the nineteenth asterism will be your Trijanma Nakshatra. These three asterisms are crucial components that are considered during the matchmaking of a bride and groom.

The nine asterisms starting from your birth star represent nine facets of human life, including Janma, Sampat, Vipat, Kshema, Pratyaka, Sadhana, Vata, Mitra, and Parama Mitra. Furthermore, the first nine nakshatras are referred to as the first pariraya, the second nine are called the second pariraya, and the third set of nine asterisms is called the third pariraya. This point plays an important during horoscope matching.

Two main types of relationships can be formed while matching horoscopes, namely Uttama (Best Relationships) and Madhyama (Moderate Relationships). The nakshatras of the boy and the girl are taken into consideration. The astrologer starts the count from the girl's Janma Nakshatra and counts until the boy's Janma Nakshatra.

If this count is four, six, or nine, which stands for Sadhana, Kshema, and Parama Mitra, the relationship is considered uttama or the best, and the marriage has a high chance of success. According to this counting structure, uttama relationships can be formed between the sixth, fifteenth, and 24th Nakshatras, the second, eleventh, and twentieth Nakshatras, and the ninth, eighteenth, and 27th Nakshatras.

If the count from the girl's to the boy's birth star is three, five, or seven, the relationship is believed to be bad, and the marriage proposal is rarely taken forward. More detailed layers need to be considered depending on which pariraya the Nakshatras of the girl and boy fall. In some cases, certain padas of the Nakshatras are considered good, while other padas are rejected.

The second type of relationship, called Madhyama or average, is formed when the boy's and girl's birth stars have a Janma, Anujanma, and Trijanma relationship with each other. Therefore, Madhyama relationships can be formed with the first, tenth, and nineteenth Nakshatras, the second, eleventh, and twentieth Nakshatras, and the eighth, seventeenth, and 26th Nakshatras.

An important rule is associated with the number 27, considering there are 27 Nakshatras in the Zodiac. If the count from the girl's Janma Nakshatra to the boy's is 27 and if Chandra is in the same sign for both, the marriage is likely to meet with success. However, if the Moon in the boy's Rashi Chart is in the twelfth house of the girl's Moon, the relationship will not be good.

If the girl and boy share the same Nakshatra, the following rules hold:

- **Uttama Relationships** – If the stars of both the girl and the boy are Rohini, Ardra, Magha, Hasta, Vishakha, Shravana, Uttara Bhadrapada, or Revati, the relationship will be the best or Uttama.

- **Madhyama Relationships** – If the stars of both the girl and boy are Ashwini, Krittika, Mrigashirsha, Pushya, Purvashada, or Uttarashada, the relationship will be moderate or Madhyama.

- **Atamam or Bad** – If both the girl and boy are of Bharani, Ashlesha, Swati, Jyeshta, Moola, Dhanishta, Shatabisha, or Purva Bhadrapada, the relationship is no good.

Ashtakoot Guna Milan

Ashtakoot Guna Milan is an astrological system used to match the compatibility factors between prospective brides and grooms. This method uses the Moon Chart, the Moon Sign, or Rashi and the prospective couple's birth stars to assess the compatibility between them. There are eight factors called Koots, consisting of 36 Gunas, that are taken into account while calculating the Guna, namely:

1. **Varna Koot** – This element is related to ego and reflects the individual's personality and background.

2. **Vashya Koot** – Vashya Koot is about power and relates to the power equation and controlling person between the couple.

3. **Tara Koot** – This element reflects the friendship between the Nakshatras of the bride and groom. It talks about the proximity between the two stars.

4. **Yoni Koot** – This element is all about the sexual attraction between the prospective bride and groom.

5. **Graha-Maitri Koot** – This is related to the harmony between the Rashi charts of the girl and boy.

6. **Gana Koot** – This element is connected to the temperament and behavior of the boy and girl.

7. **Bhakoot** – This element is about love and is connected to the boy's and girl's Rashi Moon positions.

8. **Nadi Koot** – This is connected to the health and genes of the prospective couple.

The weightage given to each of these factors is the same as the serial number against them, and the maximum score is 36.

The Asktakoot Guna Milan calculates the Guna and arrives at a score for the match, which can be an indicator of the marriage's future. If the score is less than eighteen, the marriage is not likely to be successful. A score between eighteen and 24 reflects an average marriage.

A score of about 24 suggests that the marriage has a high potential for success, with the couple being happy in their relationship. Scores between 25-32 are good, while those between 32 and 36 are considered exceptional, and the marriage is destined for success. Now, look at the eight Koots in more detail.

Varna Koot - The Varna is a determining factor of an individual's ego and personality according to their Zodiac sign. According to Vedic Astrology, Zodiac signs are divided into four Varnas, namely Brahmin, Kshatriya, Vaishya, and Shudra, in descending order of hierarchy.

> • Cancer (Karkata Rashi), Scorpio (Vrischika Rashi), and Pisces (Meena Rashi) belong to the Brahmin Varna

> • Aries (Mesha Rashi), Leo (Simha Rashi), and Sagittarius (Dhanush Rashi) belong to the Kshatriya Varna

> • Taurus (Vrishabha Rashi), Virgo (Kanya Rashi), and Capricorn (Makar Rashi) belong to the Vaishya Varna.

> • Gemini (Mithuna Rashi), Aquarius (Kumbh Rashi), and Libra (Tula Rashi) belong to the Shudra Varna

Marriages made between a girl and a boy within the same Varna are considered to be auspicious. If the groom's Varna is higher than the bride's, the match is considered approachable. However, if the bride's Varna is higher than the boy's, it signifies an inauspicious marriage.

Vashya Koot - This category of Guna compatibility is a reflection of who will dominate in the marriage. It is not just domination over a partner but the power of holding the reins attractively and sensibly to make a success of the marriage. Holding 2 points, this category involves Zodiac signs and their connection to five types of animals, including the following:

> • Chatushpada (translates to four-footed) - Aries, Taurus, the first half of Capricorn, and Sagittarius's second half

> • Human - Gemini, Virgo, Libra, Aquarius, and the first half of Sagittarius

> • Jalchar (water animals) - Cancer, Pisces, and the second half of Capricorn

> • Vanacara (jungle or wild animals) - Leo

- Keet (worms) – Scorpio

There is a scoring system when the Zodiac signs of the bride and groom are matched. For example, if the bride and groom both have Zodiac signs in the Chatuspada category, the score is 2—which is the maximum allocated for this Koot. There are 25 such combinations, and each combination is given a score ranging from 0 to 2.

Simply put, when both belong to the same animal category, the score is the maximum, namely 2. Score 1 is given for the following combinations:

- Bride – human, groom – chatuspada
- Bride – jalchar, groom – chatuspada
- Bride – Keet, groom – chatuspada
- Bride – Chatuspada, Groom human
- Bride – Keet, Groom – human
- Bride – Chatuspada, Groom – Jalchar
- Bride – Keet, Groom – Keet
- Bride – Jalchar, Groom – Vanacara
- Bride – Chatuspada, Groom – Keet
- Bride – Human, Groom – Keet
- Bride – Jalchar, Groom – Keet

Score 1.5 is given for the following combinations:

- Bride – Jalchar, Groom – Human
- Bride – Human, Groom – Jalchar
- Bride – Chatuspada, Groom – Vanacara

Score 0 is given for the following combinations:

- Bride – Vanacara, Groom – Chatuspada
- Bride – Vanacara, Groom – human
- Bride – Vanacara, Groom – jalchar

- Bride – Keet, Groom – Vanacara

- Bride - Vanacara, Groom – Keet

- Bride – human, Groom – Vanacara

Tara Koot – This category determines the overall destiny and well-being of the prospective couple. The 27 Nakshatras are divided into nine groups. Studying the bride's and groom's stars within the framework of this division is a good indicator of the marriage's success. Starting from the bride's star, count until the boy's Nakshatra is reached. Divide this number by 9; the remainder reflects the overall well-being of the couple. The remainder is matched against the nine life aspects discussed in the previous chapter. They are:

1. Janma - Bad

2. Sampath – Good

3. Vipat – Bad

4. Kshema – Good

5. Prayatak – Bad

6. Sadhana – Good

7. Vadha or Naidhana – Bad

8. Mitra – Good

9. Parama Mitra – Good

For example, if the count from the girl's star to the boy's star is 12, dividing 12 by 9 gets you a quotient of 1 and a remainder of 3. Now, 3 represents Vipat, which is bad, and therefore, the Tara Koot indicator is not good for the marriage.

Yoni Koot – The matching of this prospective couple's aspect is the most popular in matching horoscopes for marriages. This Koot stands for the sexual energy and attraction between the girl and boy. Nakshatras are given animal symbols that reflect each asterism's sexual behavior. The sexual compatibility is achieved by comparing the animals projected by both the girl's and boy's birth stars.

The five animals include:

1. Swabhava Yoni

2. Friend or Mitra Yoni

3. Neutral Yoni

4. Opposite Yoni

5. Enemy Yoni

The sexual compatibility is the best in the Swabhava Yoni pair because both the bride and the groom share the same class of Yoni. It is easy to understand that the least compatible pair is the Enemy pair because each of the partners belongs to an entirely different yoni class. Now, look at the classification of Nakshatras based on Yoni and use examples to explain the pairs:

- Ashwini and Shatabhisha belong to the Ashwa (horse) class of Yoni

- Bharani and Revati belong to the Gaja (elephant) class of Yoni

- Pushya and Kritika belong to the Mesha (sheep) class of Yoni

- Rohini and Mrigashirsha belong to the Sarpa (serpent) class of Yoni

- Moola and Ardra belong to the Shwan (dog) class of Yoni

- Ashlesha and Punarvasu belong to the Marjara (cat) class of Yoni

- Magha and Purva Phalguni belong to the Mushaka (rat) class of Yoni

- Uttara Phalguni and Uttara Bhadrapada belong to the Gau (cow) class of Yoni

- Swati and Hasta belong to the Mahisha (buffalo) class of Yoni

- Vishakha and Chitra belong to the Vyaghra (tiger) class of Yoni

- Jyeshtha and Anuradha belong to the Mriga (deer) class of Yoni

- Purvashada and Shravana belong to the Vanara (monkey) class of Yoni

- Uttarashada and Abhijeet belong to the Nakul (mongoose) class of Yoni

- Purva Bhadrapada and Dhanishta belong to the Singha (lion) class of Yoni

Natives belonging to the same class of Yoni are sexually more compatible than natives belonging to different classes. For example, if the bride and groom are of Moola and Ashlesha Nakshatra, respectively, their Yoni classes would be dog and cat, which are natural enemies. Therefore, their sexual compatibility from their horoscopes' point of view will not be good at all.

Graha-Maitri Koot – This element in the Ashtakoot Guna Milan system is used to determine the mutual love and respect and mentality of a prospective couple. This element is also a measure of the partners' willingness to work together to make the marriage successful. This element's score will help you determine whether you and your prospective spouse will agree with each other more or disagree.

This aspect is studied in detail by reading into the planet lords of the prospective bride's and groom's Zodiac signs. If the Rashis of the bride and groom are ruled by friendly planets and belong to the same Moon sign, the pair is expected to be highly compassionate and understanding of each other.

Contrarily, if enemy planets rule the Zodiac signs of the bride and the groom, this element's score will be low, and the marriage would not be an approachable one. The maximum points for this element are 6.

Gana Koot – This element determines the basic characteristic of a person. Nakshatras are divided into three categories, namely Devta, Manushya, and Rakshasa Gana. These categories represent three different natures or behavioral attitudes of the native. For example, a person from the Devta Gana would be patient and gentle in their behavior. An individual from the Rakshasa Gana would be inconsiderate, rude, aggressive, but straightforward. A person from the Manushya Gana would be somewhere between these two. They would be gentle but ready to become aggressive if the situation demanded it. Here are the Nakshatras and their respective Ganas:

- Devta Gana – Ashwini, Mrigashirsha, Punarvasu, Pushya, Hasta, Swati, Anuradha, Shravana, and Revati
- Manushya Gana – Bharani, Rohini, Ardra, Purva Phalguni, Uttara Phalguni, Purvashada, Uttarashada, Purva Bhadrapada, and Uttara Bhadrapada
- Rakshasa Gana – Krittika, Ashlesha, Magha, Chitra, Vishakha, Jyeshtha, Moola, Dhanishta, and Satabhisha

Bhakoot Koot – Also referred to as Rashi Koot, this element of the Ashtakoot Guna Milan system is allocated 7 points. The moon signs, and the placement of Chandra in the Rashi Charts of the prospective couple, are taken into consideration for this Koot. These two aspects are analyzed and evaluated for their strengths and weaknesses.

If the bride and groom's birth sign is 6-8, Shadashtak Yoga is considered to be formed. In this Yoga, if the planet lords of the two Moon signs are natural enemies, the marital life is likely to be full of problems and sufferings. Financial problems, accidents, and problems from direct and indirect enemies are likely to bring suffering to the married couple.

Dwidwadash dosha is when a combination of 2-12 is obtained when comparing the bride's and groom's birth signs. If the combination is 5-9, Navapancham Dosha is formed. The Navapancham Dosha makes the groom have a sense of detachment from the real world.

Contrarily, if the bride's moon sign is 9 when counted from the groom's moon sign, the bride might tend to abandon the world. However, if the planets of both moon signs are friendly, this situation could settle down.

Full points, 7, is given if the bride's and groom's Moon signs are the same or if the moon of both is on the 1/7, 3/11, and 4/10 axes. This Guna gets 0 points if the moon is on the 2/12, 5/9, and 6/8 axis.

Nadi Koot – The 27 Nakshatras are categorized into three types, namely Aadi, Madhya, and Antya Nadi. These are collectively called Nadi Milan or Nadi Dosha. With 8 points, this Koot is an important element to consider for matching the horoscopes of the bride and groom.

Nadi should be different for the bride and groom for the horoscopes to get a go-ahead for marriage. If they are the same, the marriage will not be a good one because the children of this marriage could suffer from health problems. While the same Nadi couples should not be considered for marriage, if the Nakshatras of the bride and groom are different, the same Nadi can be considered. Matching Nadi Koot is a complex and layered process.

According to Vedic Astrology, a marriage between a bride and groom, both belonging to Devta Gana Nakshatras, would be highly auspicious. A marriage between a groom from the Rakshasa Gana and a bride from the Devta Gana would be very inauspicious and unstable. Ideally, people from the same Gana should be chosen as partners.

Lastly, while the Ashtakoot Guna Milan score gives a reasonable, clear picture of marriage prospects, it is not sufficient by itself. Other astrological factors should also be considered before arriving at a final decision. Expert astrologers believe that the scores can be taken as a good indicator but should never be taken in isolation. The other factors to be considered along with the Ashtakoot Guna Milan scores include:

- The Lagna of the bride and groom
- The strength of the ascendant and that of its ruler
- The strength of the seventh house and its ruler
- The strength and nature of Jupiter and Venus
- The natural friendship/relationship between the rulers of the Lagna and the seventh house
- All the Nakshatra positions that deal with mental, physical, and financial compatibility of the bride and groom

Venus specifically requires special attention because this planet's strength and weakness play an important role in a marriage's success or failure. Inauspicious placement of Venus in the boy's horoscope can cause infertility. In a girl's horoscope, Jupiter plays a crucial because it reflects the house of the husband. Its strength and weakness can be a good indicator of the future of marriage.

You can also see how Nakshatras and other aspects of Vedic Astrology can help you determine a good partner for yourself. The next chapter deals with career planning.

Chapter 8: Nakshatras and Career Planning

Career Planning is another important topic in Predictive Vedic Astrology. Career planning is a crucial aspect of life, and Vedic Astrology can be a highly useful tool to see the direction and path that your career is likely to take. The native's Nakshatra and its lord are powerful indicators of the career path. Now, look at each of the Nakshatras and their inspiration toward natives' professions.

Ashwini – the Star of Transport

Ashwini, located in Mesha Rashi and ruled by Ketu, is known as the Star of Transport. Ketu renders a mystical and mysterious aura to the life journey of a native born in Ashwini. The symbol of this asterism, a horse's head, is a powerful indicator of the adventurous spirit combined with a headstrong personality of Ashwini natives.

The ruling gods are the Ashwin twins, who ride in a golden chariot showering healing power to Earth's mortals. The Ashwin twins are referred to as the "Physicians to the Gods." Their healing and revitalizing powers form the crux of their strength. They heal people and help them reach their goals and achieve their dreams.

Ashwini Nakshatra has a Devata Guna (godly temperament), and they are motivated by dharma. The career interests of natives born in Ashwini Nakshatra are usually:

- Therapists and psychologists
- Mystic healers and physicians
- Law enforcement agency workers, including military
- Travel agents and other travel and transportation-related jobs
- Athletes, jockeys, and horse trainers

Bharani – the Star of Restraint

Covered by the Aries Zodiac, Bharani Nakshatra is ruled by Venus or Shukra. The symbol is a yoni or clay vessel. This symbol reflects Bharani's potent creative energy, considering it is ruled by Venus, the representative power of sexual energy and creativity.

The ruling deity is Yama, the Lord of Death. Interestingly, in the Atharva Veda, Bharani is listed as the last Nakshatra, symbolizing the end of things and life. Bharani is also known as Apabharani, which translates to "water that carries away things."

This power symbolizes the potential to remove and cleanse impurities. With a manushya temperament, Bharani's primary motive is prosperity or artha (wealth). The career interests of Bharani-born natives are:

- Writers, publishers, and jobs in the film and music industry
- Occultists, hypnotists, astrologers, and psychologists
- Business entrepreneurs, building contractors, and financial consultants
- Careers and jobs in the hotel industry, including catering, chef, etc.

- Careers related to births and deaths, such as fertility specialists, morticians, workers in funeral homes, and gynecologists.

- Politicians, lawyers, and judges

Krittika – the Star of Fire

Ruled by Surya, and with Agni (the Lord of Fire) as the ruling deity, Krittika's symbol is the primordial flame, representing purification through yagna or the sacrificial fire. This Nakshatra's power is to "burn away" ignorance and negativity to reveal the underlying truth. It has a Rakshasa nature, and the primary motive is desire or kama. The career interests of Krittika-born natives are:

- Heads of states, advisors, and spiritual teachers

- Fashion designers, models, musicians, artists, singers, and dancers

- Weapon makers, military personnel, and building contractors

- Potters, cooks, Vedic priests, and other professions involving fire

Rohini – the Star of Ascent

Chandra rules Rohini, and the ruling deity is Brahman, the creator. Rohini has many symbols, including a temple, chariot, and banyan tree. This Nakshatra's power represents a movement toward the divine (temple). The banyan tree is considered sacred and the home of the Goddesses of the Indus Valley Civilization. With a manushya temperament, the primary motivation for Rohini is spiritual liberation. Careers for Rohini natives are:

- Models, actors, and fashion designers

- High positions in the hotel industry

- Careers in food products, agriculture, real estate, and herbal market

- Consultants and politicians

Mrigashirsha – the Searching Star

Mrigashirsha is ruled by Mars and has the symbol of a deer's face. This Nakshatra has a devta temperament, and spiritual liberation is the primary motivation. Mars, its ruling planet, represents the energy of a spiritual warrior. This is a great constellation for research of philosophical and spiritual pursuits. Careers of Mrigashirsha natives include:

- Teachers, researchers, actors, writers, and poets

- Mystics, astrologers, and psychics

- Gemologists and engineers

- Animal trainers and veterinary doctors

- Careers in the travel industry, real estate, and business development

Ardra – the Star of Sorrow

The main symbol of Ardra is a human head. It is ruled by Rahu, who represents thinking. The second symbol of Ardra is a teardrop, which reflects the power to overcome suffering. Ardra is a Nakshatra associated with brilliant mental ability and represents emotional cleansing that happens after suffering. Ardra career interests include:

- Careers in hospitals, hospice cares, and pain management

- Teachers, writers, social service workers, and public relations

- Careers in humanitarian projects and politics

- Mathematics, atomic research, and engineering
- Drug dealers, butchers, chemists

Punarvasu – the Star of Renewal

This illuminating asterism has a bow and a quiver of arrows as its symbol. The meaning of Punarvasu is "the return of the light." This star's power lies in its ability to restore the light of spirituality into the darkness of ignorance. It also stands for moral values, purity, and truth. The strength of this Nakshatra is the ability to gain abundance and wealth. Punarvasu is ruled by Jupiter, the greatest of benefic planets. Career interests include:

- Careers in the entertainment industry, including acting, drama, etc.
- Directors, publishers, and writers
- Psychologists, mystics, spiritual teachers, and philosophers
- Civil engineers, architects, inventors, and scientists
- Social workers and politicians

Pushya – the Star of Nourishment

Pushya is considered to be the most auspicious Nakshatras among all the 27. It has various symbols, including a circle, lotus, arrow, and, most particularly, a cow's udder. With a deva temperament, the primary motivation for Pushya is dharma, or rightful action and living. Saturn, its ruling planet, offers stable grounding for this asterism. The power of Pushya is the ability to create spiritual energy. Career interests include:

- Careers in politics and governments
- Careers in the police, military, and law
- Artists, poets, and musicians

- Careers in the dairy industry and geology
- Spiritual and religious teachers

Ashlesha – the Clinging Star

A coiled serpent is the symbol of this intense asterism. The coiled serpent represents the immense potential of Kundalini energy residing at the base of the spine. Ashlesha translates to "entwine" and denotes the challenges of human beings to be excessively attached to sensory and materialistic pleasures. The power of Ashlesha is the ability to spout venom. With a Rakshasa temperament, people born in Ashlesha Nakshatra are driven by dharma. Career interests are:

- Teachers, writers, lawyers
- Zoologists and other animal-related studies
- Mystics, astrologers, and psychics
- Careers in business development and speculative ventures, including the stock market
- Chemists, drug dealers, gamblers
- Addiction counselors and sex therapists

Magha – the Star of Power

Magha means "the mighty one." This asterism stands for strength and spiritual leadership. Ruled by Ketu, Magha's symbol, which has a Rakshasa temperament, is the king's palanquin or bed. The primary motivation of people born under Magha is material prosperity or artha. The power of Magha is "the ability to leave the body." Career interests include:

- Business entrepreneurs and self-employment
- Researchers, historians, and archeologists
- Careers in the field of drama and cinema

- Heads of corporations, lawyers, and politicians

Purva Phalguni – the Fruit of the Tree

Purva Phalguni is ruled by Venus and is known for its creative power. People born in this sign are usually skilled in the fine arts and love pleasurable pursuits driven by their primary motivation, namely kama or desire. The symbol of this asterism is a couch, swinging hammock, or two legs of a bed – all three reflect a place and time of enjoyment and rest. Purva Phalguni has a manushya temperament and is known for "the power of creative procreation." Career interests include:

- Careers in photography, radio, and television
- Artists, musicians, actors, and models
- Travel agents and careers in retail sales
- Wedding planners and jobs in jewelry and cosmetics
- Politicians and government service
- Marital and sex therapists

Uttara Phalguni – the Star of Patronage

The symbol of this asterism is a healing bed or the two legs of a cot. It is a service-oriented Nakshatra and is ever ready to help a friend in need. Uttara Phalguni star people possess excellent healing skills and can find harmony in careers related to healing and counseling. With a manushya temperament, the main motivation for this asterism is spiritual liberation. The power of Uttara Phalguni is "the ability to give prosperity through marriage." Career interests include:

- Philanthropists, social workers, and careers in charitable work
- State health officials and careers in the healing art

- Actors, writers, and media personnel

- Mathematicians, astrologers, and astronomers

- Business entrepreneurs and jobs in public relations and sales

Hasta

The symbol of Hasta Nakshatra is the hand or palm. The ruling deity is Savitar, the creative form of Surya. The power of Hasta is "the capability to manifest what the seeker seeks and put it in their hands." Hasta natives are known for excellent dexterity with their hands and are good with handicrafts and healing arts. With a devta temperament, the primary motivation of Hasta Nakshatra is spiritual liberation. Career interests include:

- Artists, painters, and craftsmen

- Teachers, scholars, performers, comedians, and writers

- Careers in voluntary work and hospitals.

- Careers in public relations

- Ministers, advisers, psychotherapists, and counselors

- Careers in networking and communication

- Conference planners and travel-related jobs

Chitra – the Star of Opportunity

Chitra means "the beautiful one," and its symbol is a pearl or bright jewel. The power of this asterism is the "ability to organize and arrange things aesthetically and artistically." The power of this Nakshatra is also "to accumulate good karma." With a rakshasa nature, the primary motivation for Chitra Nakshatra is kama. Career interests of Chitra Nakshatra are:

- Jewelers, clothing and fashion designers

- Interior designers and architects

- Judges, lawyers, priests

- Careers in religious fields related to the knowledge of scriptures

- Careers in creative business and the field of art and music

- Writers, publishers, TV, films, and radio

Swati – the Self-Motivated Star

Ruled by Rahu, the symbol for Swati Nakshatra is a single blade of grass blowing in the wind. This symbol reflects the autonomous and independent nature of this constellation. People born in this star love traveling for education and learning. They are always yearning to make positive changes. Swati's primary power is its "capability to scatter things in the wind," considering its ruling deity is Vayu, the Wind God. With a devta temperament, another symbol for Swati is a sword reflecting the power of accurate discrimination. Career interests include:

- Entrepreneurs and independent business owners

- Positions of leadership

- Careers in sales, travel, and the transportation industry

- Meditation and yoga teachers

- Careers in the legal profession, including lawyers, judges, etc.

- Drug and alcohol traders, stockbrokers

Vishakha – the Star of Purpose

Jupiter rules Vishakha, and its ruling deity is Agni. The power of this Nakshatra is its "ability to obtain different fruits in life." The symbol is an archway or a potter's wheel. The archway represents the threshold of a spiritual journey. The potter's wheel is a reflection of the patience needed to succeed in the spiritual path. Career interests are:

- Public speakers, teachers, writers
- Scientists and researchers
- Lawyers and politicians
- Dictators, military leaders
- Ambassadors of humanitarian work

Anuradha – the Star of Success

The ruling planet of Anuradha is Saturn, which gives discipline and tenacity during difficult times. Its symbol is a lotus, which reflects its capability to blossom regardless of the external circumstances. Its ruling deity is Mitra, the Lord of Partnership and Friendship. People born in this Nakshatra are skilled at gathering people together for both social and spiritual activities.

With a devta temperament, the primary motivation of Anuradha Nakshatra is dharma. Its primary power lies in the "ability to worship." Career interests include:

- Careers in business management
- Planners and organizers
- Careers in the travel industry
- Public speakers, musicians, and actors
- Plumbers and mining engineers
- Politicians and criminal lawyers

Jyeshta – the Elder or Chief Star

Jyeshtha translates to "senior-most" or "eldest." The symbols for this asterism are an umbrella and earring. The latter represents Lord Vishnu's discus, while the umbrella symbolizes status and protection. Jyeshtha has a rakshasa nature, and its primary motivation is the accumulation of wealth. The power of this constellation is its "ability to rise and conquer in battle through courage and bravery." Career interests include:

- Business managers and self-employment
- Dancers, musicians, and models
- Philosophers, researchers, and intellectuals
- Police detectives and military leaders
- Engineers and careers in exploration and mining

Moola – the Foundation Star

Moola means "the root or foundation." Its symbol is a bunch of roots tied together. The ruling planet is Ketu, which reflects a sense of mysticism to this constellation. The ruling deity is Nirritti, the Goddess of Destruction, connected to Kali, the all-powerful destroyer of evil. The power of Moola is the "ability to destroy, ruin, and break things." It is a rakshasa Nakshatra, and its primary motivation is Kama. Career interests include:

- Spiritual teachers, philosophers, and ministers
- Writers and public speakers
- Politicians and lawyers
- Business entrepreneurs
- Careers in sales
- Healers, doctors, and pharmacists

Purvashada – the Invincible Star

Purvashada translates to "early victory" or the "undefeated." Ruled by Venus, the symbol of this asterism is a winnowing basket or fan that can rid the corn from its husk. The ruling deity is Apas, the Cosmic Waters. The power of this Nakshatra is in its capability to invigorate. With a manushya temperament, the primary motivation of Purvashada is spiritual liberation. Career interests are:

- Careers in the boating and shipping industry
- Debaters, teachers, writers, and public speakers
- Careers in foreign trade and travel industry
- Careers in the film industry as actors and directors
- Politicians and lawyers

Uttarashada – the Universal Star

The meaning of Uttarashada is "later victory." Its symbol is an elephant tusk associated with Lord Ganesha, the remover of obstacles. It has a second symbol, the planks of a bed, which signifies peace, rest, and security. Uttarashada has a manushya temperament, and its primary motivation is spiritual liberation. The power of this asterism is "the ability for unchallengeable victory." Career interests include:

- Social workers and government servants
- Innovators and pioneers
- Researchers, healers, and scientists
- Hunters and careers in the military
- Fighters who fight for a cause

Shravana – the Star of Learning

Shravana means "to listen," and therefore, its primary symbol is an ear. With a devta temperament, Shravana's power is in its ability to hear the astral sounds from Lord Krishna's flute, the cosmic Om, and the celestial bells. People born in this star usually have brilliant minds and can easily study other cultures and spiritual dimensions. Their primary motivation is the creation of wealth. Career interests include:

- Speech therapists, teachers, and linguists
- Religious priests, scholars, and astrologers
- Careers in business, politics, geology
- Researchers and professors
- Careers in the travel industry

Dhanishta – the Star of Symphony

Also referred to as the "kingly star," people under the influence of Dhanishta can earn much fame and wealth. Its symbol is the drum, which reflects a love for music. With a rakshasa temperament, people born in this asterism are likely to be challenged by a fiery temper and marriage difficulties. Career interests include:

- Drummers, poets, and musicians
- Surgeons and doctors
- Careers in property management and real estate
- Careers in mining and engineering
- Researchers and scientists
- Careers in humanitarian work and charitable projects

Shatabisha - the Hundred Stars

Shatabisha also translates to "the hundred flowers" or "the hundred healers." Its symbol is an empty circle, which reflects an independent and autonomous character. The ruling deity is Varuna, the God of Water and Medicine, which is why natives born in this asterism have a strong connection to the healing arts. The power of Shatabisha is "the ability to heal." Shatabisha has a Rakshasa temperament, and its primary motivation is dharma or rightful action. Career interests are:

- Astronomers and astrologers
- Nurses, physicians, and healers
- Researchers, writers, and nuclear scientists
- Careers in the clerical industry, including secretaries and editors
- Electricians and engineers
- Careers in organizational capacities and business skills

Purva Bhadrapada – the Burning Pair

This asterism has three symbols: a two-faced man, the front two legs of a funeral cot, and a sword. The two-faced man and the two legs represent the power of the natives born in this asterism to see both sides of an issue. The sword represents the power to slice through negativity to get to the ultimate truth. The primary power of Purva Bhadrapada is "the ability to lift an individual in his or her spiritual life." With a manushya temperament, the primary motivation for these asterisms is the accumulation of wealth. Career interests include:

- Careers in business and administration
- Researchers and statisticians
- Ascetics, priests, and idealistic visionaries

- Occultists, astrologers, tantric
- Careers in geriatric field, hospice work, and nursing

Uttara Bhadrapada – the Warrior Star

The symbol of the Uttara Bhadrapada is represented by the back two legs of a funeral cot. Another symbol is a pair of twins. The word "Bhadrapada" means "scorching" or "burning pair." It connects the twin Nakshatras of Purva and Uttara Bhadrapada. With a manushya temperament, the primary motivation for this asterism is a pleasure. Career interests include:

- Careers in non-profit and charitable organizations
- Careers in the travel industry and import-export
- Saints, religious careers like priests and priestess, mystics, and astrologers
- Philosophers, writers, researchers, and teachers

Revati – the Wealthy Star

The symbols for Revati are a drum and fish. The drum is a marker of time signifying the last constellation in the Zodiac. The fish represents deep spirituality. This Nakshatra has a devta temperament, and the primary motivation is spiritual liberation. The power of Revati is "the power to nourish." Revati is considered one of the most beneficial asterisms for developing psychic abilities and spiritual growth. Career interests include:

- Careers in charitable and humanitarian causes
- Animal trainers and vets
- Publishers, editors, and journalists
- Government services, social work, and urban planners
- Careers in the travel industry, including flight attendants

In Vedic Astrology, every aspect of life, including careers, can be determined by reading deeply into the native's divisional charts. Unlike Western Astrology, which only looks at the Zodiac sign of an individual to predict career paths, Vedic Astrology covers a wide horizon of factors that affect this aspect of your life.

Your Nakshatra, the symbols they represent, the ruling deities, the ruling planets, the positional aspect of the planets to each other—both on the Zodiac and on the concerned individual's divisional charts—and many more determinants are taken into account to find the right bill in terms of career. In comparison, methods used by Western Astrology appear insufficient and superficial.

The indicators given in this chapter are only a form of guidance. Feel free to consult a reputed astrologer and seek help if you want to delve into your career-changing plans. Having a strong basic idea will help you understand your life's career path even as you seek a professional's guidance.

Chapter 9: The Muhurta: Electional Astrology

Muhurta or Electional Astrology—also known as event astrology—is based on the concept of Nakshatras and involves determining what the best time for an event is based on the astrological auspiciousness of that time. It plays an important part in all Indian households because the start of any crucial event sets the pace for the event's success or failure. Again, Nakshatras and its various connected aspects, including directions, natures, and others, fix auspicious times for events—a topic referred to as Electional Astrology.

Understanding the Concept of Muhurta

Muhurta has multiple connotations and definitions. Interestingly, Abhijeet Nakshatra—the 28th one that is not considered for other aspects of predictive astrology—plays an important role in Muhurtha. Read on to learn more.

Muhurta is a measure of time used in Hindu calendars. The duration of a muhurta is 48 minutes counted from the time of sunrise. It is important to note here that according to the Hindu calendar known as Panchanga System, a day of 24 hours is measured from sunrise to sunrise and not from midnight.

The smallest time unit known to ancient India's seers is called a "Nimisha," which is considered the smallest unit of time conceivable by human beings. "Nimisha" is defined as "the blink of an eye." This is a linear concept and a fixed measure. The bigger measurements of time are:

- Fifteen nimisha equals one kashta

- Fifteen kashta equals one laghu

- Fifteen laghu equals one ghatika (another name for ghatika is "danda")

- Two ghatika (or 30 laghu) equals one muhurta

- 30 muhurta equals one divai-ratri (24 hours)

Astrologically, one muhurta is not taken exactly as 48 minutes every day. This value varies depending on the local moon, sunrise, and sunset. It is a non-linear, cyclical concept, and therefore, is not fixed. One sidereal day and night—referred to as "nakshatra ahoratra"—has 30 muhurtas. Each sidereal day and night is divided into four time zones—called Praharas, each of seven and one-third muhurtas—as follows:

- The time between sunrise and noon is the first Prahara

- The time between noon and sunset is the second Prahara

- The time between sunset and midnight is the third Prahara

- The time between midnight and the next sunrise is the fourth Prahara

The four points in time, namely sunrise, noon, sunset, and midnight are called Gayatri pada. Therefore, four Praharas make 24 hours. The Abhijeet Muhurta, which is the last half Muhurta in the first Prahara and the first half Muhurta in the second Prahara, is considered very auspicious as it is mapped to the Abhijeet Nakshatra ruled by Lord Hari.

The seven Nakshatras before Abhijeet, namely Swati, Vishakha, Anuradha, Jyeshtha, Magha, Purva Phalguni, and Uttara Phalguni, constitute the remaining seven Muhurtas in the first Prahara. The balance of twenty Nakshatras then fits into the twenty Muhurtas of the remaining three Praharas after the Abhijeet Muhurta. Thus, all the 28 Nakshatra fit into the 28 Muhurtas of each day. The remaining two Muhurtas of the day—totaling 96 minutes before sunrise—are attributed to the God of Creation, Brahma, and, therefore, is loosely referred to as Brahma Muhurta.

However, the last two Muhurtas have different energies and are better associated with different deities. The 29th—the second last one—is attributed to Brahma, and the last one belongs to Surya, or Savitur, the Sun God's creative form. Lord Brahma is the ruling deity of Saturn and is related to the rebirth of the soul, which is why the 29th Brahma Muhurta is great to meditate on your Creator.

The last Muhurta is excellent for seeking the blessings of Savitur to direct your intelligence to the correct path. Each of the other Muhurtas of the day has its own significance.

Selection of the Muhurta

The following factors are taken into consideration during Muhurta selection, which consists of the day and time to undertake events:

- The tithi (or the Lunar Day)
- Nakshatra (the asterism in which Chandra is placed on that day)
- The Yoga Karana (or the auspiciousness of the chosen time)
- Vara (the weekday)

In addition to the above, certain times during the day are considered good/bad, and certain combinations of Nakshatras and weekdays are considered good/bad, etc. These considerations also need to be taken into account before selecting the Muhurta.

The Thithi

There are 30 thithis in a lunar month divided into two fortnights, each starting from the new moon day and the full moon day. In addition to being the lunar date, a thithi is a measure of the Sun and Moon's separation. Each Thithi has its own planetary lord, and people born in different thithis have varying characteristics. For example, a person born on the full moon day (Poornima) has stronger characteristic traits than one born on a new moon day (amavasya). The thithis are divided into five types:

1. **Ananda (Joyous) Thithis** – Prathipada (the first day of the fortnight), Shasti (the sixth day), and Ekadashi (the eleventh day) form the full moon or amavasya day. These days bestow joy and happiness.

2. **Mangala Thithis** – Also known as Bhadra, Arogya, or healthy thithis, these include Dwitiya (the second day), Saptami (the seventh day), and Dwadashi (the twelfth day). These days are good for starting new work.

3. **Jaya Thithis** – Jaya means victory, and the days include Tritiya (the third day of a fortnight) that falls on a Tuesday, Ashtami (the eighth day), and Trayodashi (the thirteenth day). These days are good for winning over rivals and enemies.

4. **Rikkta Thithis** – Also known as Nashta or Loss thithis, these lunar days include Chaturthi (the fourth day) falling on a Saturday, Navami (the ninth day), and Chaturdashi (the fourteenth day). These days are not good to undertake any important work or event –they should be completely avoided.

5. **Poorna Thithis** – Also known as Sampoorna days, these thithis include Panchami (the fifth day falling on a Thursday), Dashami (the tenth day), and Amavasya or Poornima (the fifteenth day of the fortnight. These are good for doing all activities.

Additionally, times such as Rahukalam, Gulika Kalam, and Yamagandam that happen every day should be avoided while fixing the Muhurta for auspicious events. The days of the week (Vara) have their important elements to consider. Now, look at them in more detail.

Vara or Weekday

Sunday – Sunday is known as Adivaram and Bhanuvaram as it is related to the Sun God, Surya, who is also known as Aditya. Adivaram is a day of life and a day filled with pure consciousness. It is a day to enjoy life, the power of the sun, and focus on the inner self. Sunday is a good day for work related to gold, trees, copper, nature, fire, silk, and coronation. On this day, controlling your temper and ego yields good karma, and it is also important not to be rude or lazy.

Monday – Known as Somavaram, this day is dedicated to the Moon or Chandra. It is a day of original thinking, creativity, and intuition. It's good for purchasing new items, including jewelry, clothes, and others. It's also a good day to conduct marriages, make intuitive decisions, and make changes with elements related to your mother, milk, and water. It's important not to be rigid and tough on Mondays. Moreover, it's not good for hair cutting, a manicure, and other barber- or parlor-related activities.

Tuesday – Tuesday or Mangalvaram is dedicated to Mars or Mangala. It is a day for material things and good for work related to metals, minerals, fire, medicine, sporting activities, and electricity. It's not a good day to start new things. It's better to avoid traveling on Tuesdays. You must take care and beware of quarrels, injuries, accidents, and falls on Tuesdays.

Wednesday – Known as Bhuddhavaram, it is a day dedicated to Mercury or Bhuddh. It's a day of knowledge, wisdom, and happiness. It's a good day for all kinds of refined work, including sales, business, shopping, starting new projects, communicating, gaining knowledge, taking medicines, marriages, and more. It's best if you avoid lying and being cruel and violent on Wednesdays.

Thursday – Called Guruvaram, according to the Vedic Calendar, Thursday is dedicated to Jupiter or Guru. It is a day of knowledge, wisdom, devotion, money, and children. It's a highly favorable day for all kinds of activities such as marriages, charitable work, gifts, shopping for important things, trading, planning finances, and starting new things in your life. You must not get angry, be greedy, lazy, or violent on Thursdays.

Friday – Friday or Shukravaram is dedicated to Venus or Shukra. It is a day of pleasures, love, harmony, fine arts, happiness, and good fortune. It's good for purchasing clothes, accessories, including jewelry, marriages, inviting and visiting friends and family, and everything else. Avoid selling important items you own on this day and being lonely.

Saturday – Dedicated to Saturn or Shani, Saturday is known as Shanivaram. It is a day of rest and recovery. It's a day for service work and charity. Taking rest on Saturdays is considered good for longevity. It's not a good day to begin anything new. It's a good day to do activities related to housing, farming, meditation, and yoga. Do not create a fuss and be careful about your health. Avoid barber- and parlor-related activities on Saturdays.

Timing of Events and 27 Nakshatras

Rohini, Uttarashadha, Uttara Bhadrapada, and Uttara Phalguni are fixed constellations, and therefore, favorable asterisms for activities with long-term, sustained, and permanent effects including:

- Digging wells
- Laying the foundations of homes, commercial establishments, temples, and even towns and cities
- Planting trees
- Purchasing land and property
- Doing meritorious deeds
- Sowing seeds
- Deity installations

Revati, Anuradha, Chitra, and Mrigashirsha are considered gentle and soft Nakshatras, and therefore, auspicious for the following activities:

- Beginning lessons in new subjects
- Fine arts, including singing, dancing
- Making new friendships and partnerships
- For sensual pleasures, including sexual union
- Wearing new clothes
- Taking out processions
- Conducting auspicious ceremonies
- Festivities
- To undertake journeys
- For agricultural activities

Hasta, Pushya, and Ashwini Nakshatras are considered to be light and swift, and so are good for the following activities:

- Sports and exercises
- Enjoying luxurious items
- Starting new industries
- Skilled labor-related jobs
- Medical treatments
- For starting education and journeys
- Seeing and meeting friends
- Buying and selling
- To perform spiritual activities
- Fine arts-related activities
- Giving and receiving loans

Satabhisha, Swati, Punarvasu, Shravana, and Dhanishta are movable and quick asterisms, and therefore, suitable for the following activities of a temporary nature:

- Undertaking journeys and travels
- Buying vehicles
- Gardening
- Processions
- Visiting friends

Purva Bhadrapada, Purvashada, Purva Phalguni, and Bharani are cruel and fierce Nakshatras. They are good for indulging in acts of deceit and evil, including:

- Conflicts and battles
- Destructions of rivals and enemies
- Incarceration
- Poisoning
- Arson
- Activities of ill-repute

Vishakha and Krittika are mixed Nakshatras and suitable for routine activities, including those related to your home and office.

How to Find an Auspicious Muhurta

There are some very broad guidelines you can use to find an auspicious time on your own. Here is a brief explanation. You can see any Panchang and check for these details.

Thithis – Avoid Chaturdashi (fourteenth day), Dwadashi (the twelfth day, but some days are fine), Navami (the ninth day), Ashtami (the eighth day), Shasti (the sixth day), and Chaturthi (the fourth day)

Varas – Monday (Somavaram), Wednesday (Bhuddhavaram), Thursday (Guruvaram), and Friday (Shukravaram) are the best, while Tuesday (Mangalavaram), Saturday (Shanivaram), and Sunday (Adivaram) are to be avoided.

Nakshatras – Those with a downward-looking direction should be avoided. These asterisms, including Bharani, Krittika, Ashlesha, Magha, Purva Phalguni, Vishakha, Moola, Purvashada, and Purva Bhadrapada, are to be avoided while fixing Muhurtas.

Yogas – There are 27 different Panchanga Yogas defined in Vedic Astrology. The ones to be avoided for auspicious occasions are Vishakumbha, Shoola, Atigandam, Gandam, Vaidhruti, Vyatipaatam, Vajram, Parigham, and Vyaghaatam.

Karana – This stands for half lunar days, and there are eleven of them defined in the Hindu Panchanga System. The ones to avoid for auspicious occasions are Chatuspadam, Vishti, Kimstughnam, Shakunam, and Nagam.

Note that the elements discussed in Chapter 2, which deal with the nature, direction, and other elements of a Nakshatra, are employed to arrive at fixing Muhurtas for auspicious events.

Chapter 10: The K.P. System of Stellar Astrology

This bonus chapter introduces you to a new system of Astrology known as K.P. Astrology. Although derived from Vedic Astrology, the K P System is focused on the use of Nakshatras and their Cuspal Lords. Read on to find out more about this intriguing system of Nakshatra-based Vedic Astrology.

The K. P. System of Stellar Astrology got its name from its inventor, Professor Kuthur Subbarayaiyyer Krishnamurthi, who lived from 1908 to 1972. He developed this new technique of making astrological predictions, which are based on the sub-lords. The K.P. System is based on the Stellar System of predictions.

The stellar astrology system was significantly researched by Shri Gopalakrishna Rao (famously known as Meena I) and N. V. Raghava Chary (known as Meena II). This system subdivides the 27 Nakshatras into 243 parts to indicate something called the asterisms' Kaalamsa positions. Professor Krishnamurthi knew both these stalwarts intimately.

He extended the theory after working on it for numerous years and brought in further divisions. According to Professor Krishnamurthi, the twelve bhavas or houses or lordship positions are subdivided into 249 positions of sub-lord. He employed the unequal proportion of the Vimshottari Dasa System to create these subdivisions.

It is important to note that Professor Krishnamurti did not go against the grain of the traditional form of Vedic Astrology. In fact, he emphasizes the importance of getting the fundamentals of the ancient system perfectly right before venturing into the K. P. System of Stellar Astrology. Some deviations from the traditional Vedic Astrology system have been taken by the founders of K. P. System, summarized as follows.

To reiterate, there are twelve Zodiac Signs (or Rashis) and twelve Bhaavs or houses in the 360-degree elliptic, according to the traditional Jyotishya. Moreover, the 27 Nakshatras or asterisms are connected to the twelve Rashis and houses, with each star getting 13 degrees, 20 minutes in the elliptic. Therefore, every house gets two and a quarter stars, which means that parts of Nakshatra(s) spillover from or into the previous or next Sign or House.

Deviations from Vedic Astrology

The Vedic system is based on the equal house concept, which is the starting point of the deviations in the K. P. System. The K. P. System uses the Placidus System of dividing the Twelve Houses wherein each Cusp of the Twelve Houses—or the beginning of each house—is treated differently and has unique measurements.

The houses' Cusps considered important factors that play a big role in a native's life and life experiences. The measurement of a house could be less than the exact 30 degrees as proposed in Vedic Astrology. Therefore, the Cusp of that particular house will be limited. In fact, in some cases, the Cusp may be entirely missing, and in other cases, two signs might have the same Cusp.

Here is an analogy to explain why further divisions within each star's span to create subdivisions, each with a sub-lord, were needed. Suppose you have a stick that you use as a measuring tool, and you divide and make equal or unequal finite sections on this stick to record the measurements. When you start using this tool, you realize that some hitherto hidden objects or elements are falling between the markings or sections, which can give erroneous measurements. Therefore, you have to make finer subsections of each section to consider the impediments to accurate measurements.

The first sub-division of the span of a star is called Sub. These Subs are again divided into even finer portions referred to as Sub-Sub. The short form is SSL. The next level of sub-divisions is called SS4, and then SS5, and so forth. To measure these Subs and SSLs, Professor Krishnamurthi again used the Dasha system's accepted Vedic form, namely the Vimshottari Dasha System.

According to this ancient, traditional system, each of the nine planets considered in Vedic Astrology has a fixed number of years, during which its Dasha will be played. Each star's span is divided into nine parts, which become the primary Sub-Division. Until now, he followed the Vedic system. Now, he further sub-divided each of these nine parts and obtained one-ninth of a part called Sub-Sub. These sub-divisions are crucial contributing factors for increasing the accuracy of predictions.

Now, a transiting planet is variable because it is continuously moving. The other considerations are Sign-Lord and Star-Lord. The moving planet will occupy one of the nine sub-parts in the star, ruled by one of the nine planets. Therefore, each Sub has a Sub-Lord. When the divisions get finer, there are Sub-Subs, each of which will have a Sub-Sub-Lord, and so forth.

The transiting planet becomes a source of an event. The lord of the star, the sub-lord, the sub-sub-lord, and the lord of the Sign, through which the planet is transiting, will decide the course of events as indicated by the house. It is important to note that the Twelve Cusps are given the same importance as the planets. Now, every Cusp will have a Cusp-Lord, Star-Lord, and Sub-Lord. Note that the Cusp-Lord will be the Sign-Lord only.

Basic Concepts of K. P. System

An asterism has a fixed length, which is 13 degrees, 20 minutes, or 800 minutes. Each of these asterisms is further divided into nine parts or divisions. Each of these nine divisions (called sub) is again ruled by a planetary lord (called sub-lord). The first ruler is the lord of the constellation himself, followed by the sequence of the lords, according to the Vimshottari Dasha System. Each part's range or span is determined by the years allotted to the planetary lords in the Vimshottari System.

Therefore, 800 minutes is taken as 120 years, which means twenty years is equal to 800 minutes. Therefore, one year is equal to 800/120, which is equal to 20/3. The above formula is used to calculate the spans of the Sub-Lords as follows:

> • Ketu rules for seven years in the Vimshottari Dasha System. Converting that using the formula 7 * 20/3), you get 0 degrees, 46 minutes, and 40 seconds.

> • Venus or Shukra rules for twenty years. His Sub-Lord Range would be 2 degrees, 13 minutes, and 20 seconds.

> • Sun or Surya rules for six years, and therefore, his range would be 0 degrees, 40 minutes.

> • Chandra ruling for ten years would have a sub-lord range of 1 degree, 6 minutes, and 40 seconds.

> • Mars or Mangala's rule is seven years. The range of his sub-lordship is 0 degrees, 46 minutes, and 40 seconds.

• Rahu (eighteen years) has a sub-lordship range of 2 degrees.

• Jupiter or Guru (sixteen years) has a sub-lordship range of 1 degree, 46 minutes, and 40 seconds.

• Saturn of Shani (nineteen years) has a sub-lordship range of 2 degrees, 6 minutes, and 40 seconds.

• Mercury or Bhuddh (seventeen years) has a sub-lordship range of 1 degree, 53 minutes, and 20 seconds

Therefore, there are twelve signs, 27 Nakshatras, and 249 Subs. Every nine Nakshatra trine sequence consists of 83 Subs in this system. In the K. P. System, the degrees of Chandra and Rahu subs get divided two times in respect of the three trines, which means there are six more Subs, taking the final tally to 249.

Interestingly, in horary Astrology—an ancient form in which the astrologer seeks to find solutions based on the time—the seeker who raised the question asks the questioner to choose a number between 1 and 249, including both. This number given by the questioner is taken as the Lagna and the beginning of the first bhaava.

Ayanamsa is included in the K. P. System calculations and is taken as 50.2388 seconds per year.

Birth charts and horary charts are prepared using the Placidus System, or the semi-arc system. The arc is measured to calculate the Sun's time to rise on a given day at a given latitude. This arc is then divided into three equal divisions. The reason for using this concept is that the rising sun's time places it exactly on the Ascendant.

After that, the Sun transits through the twelfth, eleventh, tenth, etc., at equal intervals until sunset when it reaches the seventh house or the Descendant. In this system, the degrees computed like this are the starting point.

Signs are employed to the strength of the planets and planetary lords. A strong planet will give immediate results, whereas a weak planet takes time to render its effects. Benefic planets in positions of debilitation will act slowly. However, they will not give bad results. Malefic planets in exaltation positions cannot alter bad results to good if their effects are bad. A planet's results are based on its occupation, ownership, and nature.

Also, the planet lord offers results according to the indication given by the Nakshatra Lord in which it is posited. This indicator is more powerful than those given by the house or the planet lord himself. A planet is predominantly under the influence of the Nakshatra lord.

The K. P. System considers that planets are not naturally benefic or malefic. Planets in predominantly improving bhavas, including one, two, three, six, ten, and eleven, give good results, and in the non-improving bhavas, namely four, five, seven, eight, nine, and twelve give bad results. The inherent nature of the planets, however, remains unchanged. Results are experienced only by lords of the dasha, bhukti, and sookshama conjoined together. A Nakshatra lord's results are modified according to the specifications and indications of that planet's sub-lord. Therefore, bad bhava significators are malefic, and good bhava significators are benefic.

In the same way, it is important not to take any house or Sign to be fully malefic or benefic. For example, the sixth house is an improving bhava. *But for what?* is the question asked by the seeker. It is an improving house for getting loans, overdrafts, or service; however, the sixth house is not good for diseases, marriages, etc. The same logic holds good for all the houses. One exception to the rule is that any house twelfth to a house has a negating effect on that house.

Significance of Sub-Lords in K. P. System

So, the range of a constellation is 800 minutes, divided into unequal divisions according to the ruling years allocated to each planet. Professor Krishnamurthi was the first astrologer to have divided this 800-minute range into nine subdivisions, and further divided each of these sub-divisions into sub-sub-divisions. The Nakshatra is analogous to the Dasha periods, the bhukti is analogous to the sub-divisions, and the antardashas are analogous to the Sub-Sub-Lord.

The birth chart can be controlled by the Cusp Sub Lord, who is, in turn, controlled by the Nakshatra lord. This affects the matters determined by the Cusp. The matters dealt with in the houses are modified according to the significations of the cuspal sub lords. Therefore, in the K. P. System, the cuspal sub-lord is the deciding factor.

Therefore, to assess and evaluate questions, the matter in the query should be seen from the perspective of the particular house's cuspal sub-lord, which deals with the matter in question. As an example, the seventh house's Cusp determines the marriage-related matters of the concerned native. If you need to look at children-related matters for a native, you must see the cuspal sub-Lord position of the fifth house, and so forth. Summarily, in the K. P. System of Stellar Astrology, the Cusp of the house and the cusp's sub-lord and his significations are analyzed to make predictions.

Additionally, multiple houses play a role in the life events of a native. The K. P. System has grouped the houses that influence life events together (like a team) and called them House Groups. The primary houses and the supporting houses are combined to get the house grouping for that particular event.

For example, the primary house for good health is the first house, and the supporting house is eleven. Now, the event is promised—in this case, it means the native will enjoy good health—if the sub-lord of the primary house's Cusp signifies both the primary and supporting house. Also, any event's timing is when the planet lords of the ongoing dasha, including the mahadasha, antardasha, and pratyantardasha lords, signify the house group. So, in the example of good health, a native will enjoy good health when he or she passes through the planetary dashas signifying houses one and eleven.

It comes as no surprise that making predictions and reading horoscopes using the K. P. System of Stellar Astrology is more complex than the traditional one, considering that the starting point is the cuspal sub-lord and cannot fit into a small chapter. But the intrigue, mystery, and fascination for this sub-topic of Vedic Astrology cannot be undermined. This bonus chapter is only to trigger an interest so that you learn more about it.

Conclusion

You are likely reeling under the amount of information given in this book about Nakshatras. The data given here is well-researched and tried and tested for centuries. However, do not be disheartened, because the only reason for feeling overwhelmed is that the subject is unfamiliar. Added to that are detailed formulas and mathematical calculations.

Reread the chapters slowly, and the second time around, you will see that it gets easier to follow. Once the wall of difficulty understanding the basics of this fascinating subject falls, it is only an upward trend. You will become so absorbed in it that nothing will stop you from devouring other advanced books and master the topic as fast as you can.

A word of caution is needed at this point. The book has many practical tips for reading the meaning of Nakshatras and their related elements to understand how they work. It is important to know that by itself, this kind of general information is not complete. Every person's Rashi chart and planet transits according to the Dasha systems are individualistic and unique.

Therefore, the information you imbibe from this book must be used in conjunction with the context of individuals' birth charts and their unique Dashas. In fact, it would be a great idea for you to keep your own Rashi Chart and the Dashas developed from your birth chart ready and use it as you learn from this book.

You will be surprised to see how easy you find it to discern the good times and the bad times in your life as you see the movement of the planets through your individual Dasha system under the influence of your birth Nakshatras and other elements related to it. So, go on, read the book, and this time, keep your own Rashi chart with you.

Here's another book by Mari Silva that you might like

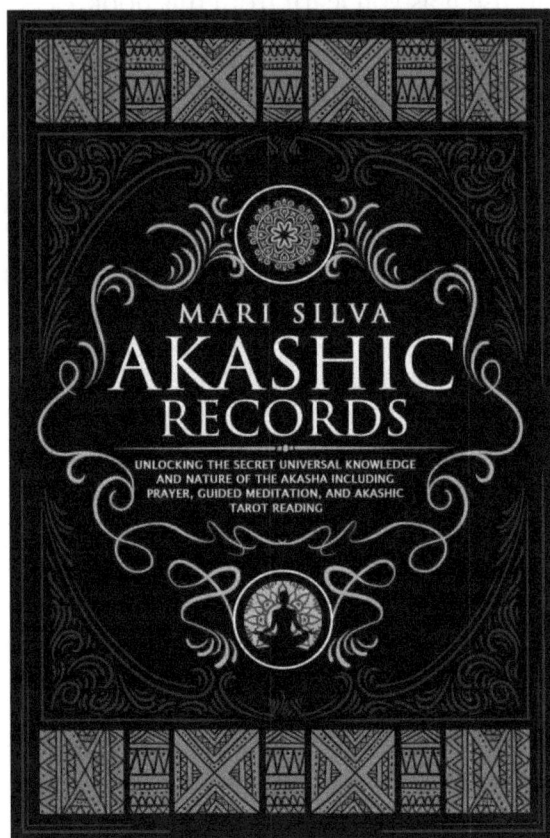

Your Free Gift (only available for a limited time)

Thanks for getting this book! If you want to learn more about various spirituality topics, then join Mari Silva's community and get a free guided meditation MP3 for awakening your third eye. This guided meditation mp3 is designed to open and strengthen ones third eye so you can experience a higher state of consciousness. Simply visit the link below the image to get started.

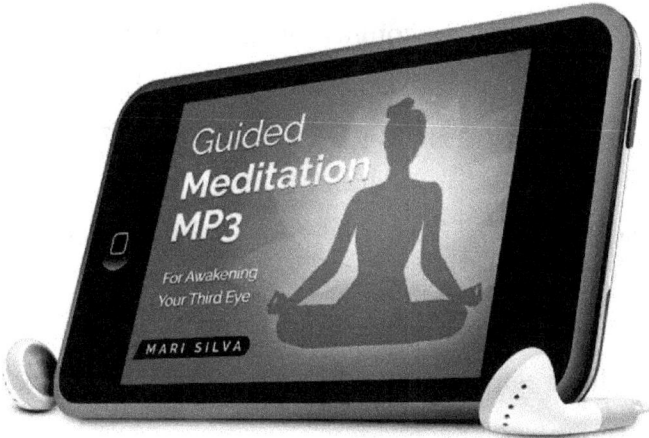

https://spiritualityspot.com/meditation

Resources

https://www.ganeshaspeaks.com/astrology/nakshatras-constellations/

https://www.astrology-prophets.com/nakshatras.php

https://www.researchgate.net/publication/313163837_28_Nakshatras_-_The_Real_Secrets_of_Vedic_Astrology_An_e-book

https://yogainternational.com/article/view/the-gunas-natures-three-fundamental-forces

https://www.dirah.org/nakshatras.htm

https://www.lunarplanner.com/Astrology/Nakshatras/index.html

https://www.astrologer-astrology.com/constellations_lords_indian_vedic_astrology_jyotish.htm

http://www.jupitersweb.com/star--sub-lord-table.html

https://www.astrojyoti.com/lesson2.htm

http://www.sarvatobhadra.com/janma-nakshatra-birth-star/

https://sites.google.com/site/familykalendars/home/chandrashtamam/janma-anujanma

https://www.astrosoftware.com/27Nakshatra.htm

https://www.selfrealisation.net/UK/VedicAstrology/symbol.htm

https://srath.com/deep-introduction-to-nakshatras/

http://divyanshraizada.blogspot.com/2019/05/nakshatras-major-element-of-vedic.html

https://www.selfrealisation.net/UK/VedicAstrology/symbol.htm

https://www.astrogle.com/astrology/animal-symbols-of-the-nakshatras.html

https://www.templepurohit.com/27-nakshatras-full-nakshatra-names-character-traits/

https://www.astrojyoti.com/phaladeepika9-4.htm

https://www.doyou.com/the-3-types-of-karma-explained/

http://astromuni.com/services/nak.asp

https://binduastrology.com/secrets-of-nakshatra-lordships-and-dasa-systems/

https://www.appliedvedicastrology.com/2018/03/04/nakshatras-secret-transits-power-nine/

https://www.boloji.com/articles/1051/dashas--a-primer

https://www.scribd.com/document/118952001/Ududasha-explanation

https://blog.indianastrologysoftware.com/dashas-and-dasha-periods/

https://www.appliedvedicastrology.com/2020/02/02/secrets-of-dashas-part-1-so-many-secret-techniques-to-get-it-right/

http://www.manyzone.com/article/11110/improve-your-nakshatras-and-stars-in-love-marriage-and-relationships

https://akashvaaniteam.blogspot.com/2018/06/8-things-ashtakoot-guna-milan-can-suggest-you-according-to-janam-kundali.html

https://www.akashvaani.com/blog/ashtakoot-guna-milan-in-a-married-life

https://astrobix.com/astrosight/192-varnadi-ashtakoot-milan-ashtakoot-milan-ashtakoot-guna-milan.html

https://rgyan.com/blogs/career-through-nakshatras-part-1/

https://wealthymatters.com/2013/11/16/nakshatras-and-careers/

https://www.astrolada.com/articles/career-astrology/find-your-career-according-to-the-27-vedic-constellations.html

http://astroworld.co.za/blog/?p=1319%22http://astroworld.co.za/blog/?p=1319

https://www.speakingtree.in/allslides/based-on-your-nakshatras-these-are-the-ideal-career-choices-for-you

https://srath.com/muhurta/

https://www.astrojyoti.com/naksatratithiyogainfo.htm

https://www.astroccult.net/general_muhurats.html

https://www.mahastro.com/how-to-easily-find-an-auspicious-muhurta-ourselves-from-any-vakya-panchangam/

https://karmicrhythms.com/how-to-fix-a-muhurtha-muhurta-panchanga-auspicious-time/

https://www.youtube.com/watch?v=fjeoLYj202I

http://stellarastrology.in/blog/category/astrology/stellar-astrology/

https://www.exoticindiaart.com/book/details/stellar-astrology-and-events-in-life-case-study-approach-to-krishnamurthy-paddhati-NAM237/

https://www.youtube.com/watch?v=HYDnFeKMn8Q

http://www.vaastuinternational.com/KP-Astrology/KP-Astrology.html

https://yogadigest.com/introduction-vedic-astrology/

https://www.astroguruonline.com/books-ancient-astrology/

https://www.speakingtree.in/blog/the-types-of-vedic-astrology

https://www.astrojyoti.com/9planets.htm

https://www.astrology-prophets.com/9-planets.php

http://www.theartofvedicastrology.com/?page_id=117

https://astrosurkhiyan.blogspot.com/2014/06/planetary-friendships.html

https://ommrudraksha.com/planet-friends-friends-and-enemies-friendship-chart-astrology

https://vicdicara.wordpress.com/2010/06/04/determining-planetary-friendship-and-enmity/

https://www.appliedvedicastrology.com/2019/08/31/the-real-meaning-of-planetary-aspects-the-nature-of-desire-in-our-chart-part-1/

http://www.theartofvedicastrology.com/?page_id=146

http://www.vaastuinternational.com/astrology4.html

https://jyotishvidya.com/bhavatbhavam.htm

http://www.bhairavastrology.com/expertise/vedic-astrology/

https://astrobix.com/astrosight/564-ayanamsa-meaning-ayanamsa.html

https://www.youtube.com/watch?v=E2AWLDwolVo

https://www.astrojyoti.com/lesson9.htm

http://www.bhairavastrology.com/expertise/vedic-astrology/

https://www.youtube.com/watch?v=NNkV9sWPVtk

http://www.theartofvedicastrology.com/?page_id=127

https://www.youtube.com/watch?v=00-PlzTA5ZQ

https://www.heerejawharat.com/astrology/astrology.php

https://www.astrojyoti.com/lesson1.htm

https://astrologer-astrology.com/zodiac_lord_indian_vedic_astrology_jyotish.htm

https://blog.indianastrologysoftware.com/study-of-divisional-charts/

http://www.theartofvedicastrology.com/?page_id=430

https://srath.com/principles-of-divisional-charts/

https://www.linkedin.com/pulse/importance-divisional-charts-vedic-astrology-pt-b-p-upadhyay

http://www.theartofvedicastrology.com/?page_id=458

https://www.dirah.org/shadbala.htm

https://vedicastroadvice.com/articles-on-vedic-astrology/shadbala_and_vedic_astrology/

https://medium.com/thoughts-on-jyotish/shadbala-the-6-sources-of-strength-4c5befc0c59a

https://www.speakingtree.in/blog/art-of-prediction-part-iii-dashas-and-transits

https://www.futurepointindia.com/article/en/timing-of-event-through-dasa-and-transit-8799

https://psychologicallyastrology.com/2019/12/23/fine-tuning-predictions-dasha-plus-transit/

https://vedicsiddhanta.in/2016/11/power-of-vimsotri-dasha-how-transits.html#.Xz1cTvlKh0w

https://astrobix.com/learn/359-determination-of-results-through-ashtakvarga.html

https://sreenivasdesabhatla.wordpress.com/2013/05/18/ashtakavarga-system-of-prediction-1/

https://www.youtube.com/watch?v=khqRo4Ujw0M

https://psychologicallyastrology.com/2019/10/12/ashtakvarga-practical-ways-of-using-the-tables/

http://circleof360.blogspot.com/2018/08/understaning-ashtakvarga-table-with.html

www.ingramcontent.com/pod-product-compliance
Lightning Source LLC
Chambersburg PA
CBHW071856090426
42811CB00004B/628